JUSTICE
NOT
CHARITY

JUSTICE NOT CHARITY

A New Global Ethic for Canada

By
Douglas Roche, M.P.

McClelland and Stewart Limited

ISBN: 0-7710-7680-0

McClelland and Stewart Limited,
The Canadian Publishers,
25 Hollinger Road,
Toronto, Ontario.
M4B 3G2

Printed and bound in Canada.

Contents

JUSTICE
NOT
CHARITY

PART ONE: THE WAY THINGS ARE

Chapter 1

The Comforts of Home

The morning after the federal budget was presented in Parliament, I was flying from Ottawa to Toronto and picked up *The Globe and Mail*. The headline of the day streamed across Page 1 in the size of type reserved for declarations of war, abdication of kings, or assassination of presidents: "Gasoline Up 15 Cents A Gallon." The subheads supplied the essential details without having to read the story:

> **"Crude oil going to $8 a barrel."**
> **"Natural gas heating to rise $65 a year."**
> **"Budget rules out compulsory controls."**

Yes, indeed a big story. I could envision gasoline at $1 a gallon soon and was secretly pleased with myself. Only the previous weekend I had persuaded my family that we really did not need that gas-guzzling station wagon we'd had the past few years and had traded it in for a Maverick.

The stewardess brought me breakfast and I continued thumbing through the paper, skimming the pages of coverage of the budget which on the whole didn't promise much sunshine. "What this budget says," the *Globe and Mail* editorial declared, "is that Canada is in deep trouble, and virtually leaderless." High food prices, new higher costs for all our energy, not enough money for new housing, higher unemployment insurance costs. Bad news, all of it.

The plane was about to land when I reached Page 16 and just as the wheels touched the ground my eye fell on this headline:

"400 million starving or badly fed, head of World Food Council says."
Rome (AP) – The World Food Council heard at its first meeting yesterday that there are 400 million starving or seriously malnourished people on the earth . . . .

A United Nations report to the Council estimated . . . over the next few years there is little prospect of a rapid reduction in the numbers of severely malnourished people . . . "

All of a sudden the distortions of modern life hit me with the force of an electric prodder.

People around me were trying to get out of their seats, but I didn't want to move. I sat there thinking of the full meaning of the juxtaposition of those two stories: the front-page news of the day revolving around the fact that we would have to pay 15 cents more for gasoline; while buried back with the ads and fashion pictures was the staggering fact that despite international food conferences, with their rhetoric and good intentions, 400 million people – eighteen times as many as in all of Canada – faced starvation.

Why wasn't the 400 million people story on Page 1 and the new gasoline tax story on Page 16? Where was the paper's sense of proportion and values? Don't be silly, I said to myself as I finally got up and headed for the terminal, the continuing suffering in a world of distorted values has become a non-story. We have been inundated with pictures of hungry children. Our compassion is exhausted. We want to put all these problems out of our mind because we have all we can do to keep things going here.

Any news editor who submerged the gasoline tax under the

hunger story would probably be fired for bad news judgement. At least the *Globe and Mail* carried a story on the World Food Council meeting. Later, I checked the newspapers of that day in ten cities across Canada. All of them blared the gas tax. The *Saint John Evening Times-Globe, Toronto Star, London Free Press, Windsor Star, Winnipeg Free Press,* and *Saskatoon Star-Phoenix* carried nothing on the Food Council. The *Ottawa Citizen* had an item on it on Page 51, the *Edmonton Journal* on Page 30, *Calgary Herald* Page 52, and *Vancouver Sun* Page 10.

Hundreds of millions of people living in the developing countries of Asia, Africa, and Latin America are caught up in conditions of deprivation that no set of statistics can begin to describe. The truth is that poverty in the developing world is an intolerable assault on human dignity and decency. Malnutrition, disease, illiteracy, unemployment, and early death pervade these vast populations.

If there is any final proof of the inhumanity of the growth ethic that has dominated the life of the industrialized nations of the West, it is the fact of one billion men, women, and children in the thirty-five least-developed nations deprived of the basics of life while the affluent nations pile up their riches. Affluent man has created more wealth than Croesus ever dreamed of. But at the expense of more misery than the world can bear. The rich squabble over gasoline prices; the poor cannot afford even fertilizer. It is a scandal beyond belief. And our insensitivity is the greatest scandal of all.

Isn't that a bit hard on Canadians? After all we're basically a modest people with no desire to exploit humanity. What's really wrong with our motivation? If we really are fat cats, as a Third World delegate to a UN conference once told me, how did we get this way and whose fault is it?

The voices of modern Canada
This jumble of thoughts about who and what we are ran through my mind a few days after my plane trip when I was standing on Parliament Hill with two of my children, watching

the July 1 celebration of Canada's birthday. This is an experience that every Canadian ought to have, at least once. Sixty thousand people jamming every square inch of Parliament Hill, waving sparklers in the early evening dusk, singing *O Canada* with all their might etches an impression of Canada on the mind that is unforgettable.

If it is not clear how much Canadians care about the world, it is clear we care about Canada. That's certainly a good beginning in the mind-stretching process of looking over the horizon.

Every so often the *Canadian Magazine* publishes letters from Canadians across the country stating what they like and don't like about the country. These snippets of feelings about bush pilots and screech, fireweed and Cape Breton Island, Sarah Binks and Bick's pickles, snow angels and Eric Nicol, Hudson's Bay blankets and Les Feux Follets, the Weeping Princess and Red Rose tea, Mme Benoit and Manitoulin are probably more revealing of our feelings than the Gallup Poll reports of what Canadians think about the super-problems or the reams of figures spewed out by Statistics Canada.

"Canada is a free country," Cheryl Campbell of Toronto wrote, "full of peace and lovely people. There is love all around you."

"Just the sound of children singing *O Canada* gives me a very big lump in my throat," said Mary Nichols of Prince George, British Columbia.

The compliments to Canada poured in to the magazine, many of them ecstatic: "Sunset over the grain elevators in a small Prairie town." "We are able to bring out our feelings in front of everybody without having to be put in prison." "I do not think there is anything like the smell of Canadian soil as the frost is coming out of the ground."

Canadians have lots of beefs too, or at least they think they do.

"My biggest beef is against foreigners in Canada," declared Ms. D. Sutton of Toronto. "The thing that makes me mad is racism," said Jenny Jessup of Weston, Ontario. "If I was a younger man, I would pick up an army from Vancouver to Winnipeg and clean that Quebec Province up right," wrote Bob Hartley of Mission City, B.C. "What makes me mad," said fifteen-year-old Daryl Mach of Grande Prairie, Alberta, "is prejudiced people."

There you have it, a mixture of joys and hopes, griefs and anxieties. What struck me in reading through page after page of the pros and cons of people's feelings about Canada was how few even referred to our relationship to the outside world. There was one notable exception from David Matheu of Toronto: "Have just finished a two-year trip through many of the Third World Countries. Please believe me, fellow Canadians, we have *everything* to be thankful for. Let's stop bitching and get together."

But getting it all together so that Canadians can decide which way we want to move is a large part of our problem. It is not only a question of raising our consciousness; we must also sort out the "information overload" that has bogged down even governments. The social-economic-political curves that the experts chart on their graphs often appear as so much mumbo-jumbo.

World energy supplies. Food shortages. Uncontrollable inflation. Over-population. Environmental destruction. Continuing mass poverty. Yet with all this Russia and the United States link up in space. The Green Revolution promises new food supplies. Nuclear energy is here and solar energy just around the corner. How can we make sense of it all? Especially when, as Duff Cornbush of West Vancouver wrote in the *Canadian*, "The leaders of our country have not told us, the citizens, where they want to lead us. This must mean that they are totally confused themselves."

And then Mr. Cornbush puts his finger on the new Canadian dilemma: "Are we to be benefactors of the world? Are we to have a large population, become an industrial nation, become multiracial, sell our assets to foreigners, or what? What are our priorities?"

In order to establish our priorities, let's take a hard look at ourselves, figuring out who and what we are.

We are a rich country

We have to begin by recognizing that by any standard, we are a rich country.

We have more telephones, cars, televisions, refrigerators, electric can-openers, single-detached homes, lawn mowers, and motor-boats than almost any other group of people in the world. Along with Americans and Western Europeans we have more schools, hospitals, libraries, and swimming pools. We earn more, spend more, eat more, and waste more than was ever imagined possible by our ancestors.

The Food Prices Review Board has concluded that "most Canadian families are spending nearly a third more for food than is necessary for a nutritious diet, yet many of them remain undernourished." And the federal Department of National Health and Welfare has mounted a campaign against what it calls "the diseases of affluence," two of which are overeating and overdrinking.

Not only do we consume more than almost anyone else, we are also sitting upon more, both literally and figuratively. With only 0.6 per cent of the world's population we have 7.3 per cent of the earth's land surface, 15 per cent of its known fresh-water resources, 17,860 miles of coastline, 10 per cent of the world's productive forest coverage, 10 per cent of its nickel, and 8 per cent of its coal. Besides these inedibles of soil and rock and wood we produce a disproportionate amount of the world's food. In short when it comes to having and getting, Canada is right up there at the front of the line.

This prodigy of affluence does not confine itself to the age-old essentials. It is certainly true that Canada dresses itself far better, eats more, and houses itself more securely than all but a few other countries. But in addition it consumes enough booze to sink ships. It smokes tons of tobacco and then spends millions of dollars in removing tumours and burying the remains. Speaking of which, this society spends more in burying its dead than many societies do in sustaining their living.

It comes as a complete surprise, therefore, to discover that there are no rich Canadians. At least, there are none who are willing to proclaim themselves rich. For example, in November 1974 the Gallup Poll asked Canadians about their "income satisfaction." While it is true that more than half – 57 per cent – replied "satisfied," more than a third muttered "dissatisfied" and a thoughtful or confused 6 per cent "could not say." These figures do not suggest a proletariat ready to storm the citadels of wealth but what is remarkable in a rich country like Canada is that no one was moved to answer "more than satisfied. I make more than I need. Please help cart it away." So far as we know few if any Canadians had trouble accepting their incomes.

Take another example. In September 1974 several thousand Canadians were asked to indulge the all-time favourite fantasy. "If your income were to increase a lot which of these would you do first?" Given a choice, as they were, you might guess that a materialistically-sated people would rebel against the offered categories and provide such spiritual answers as, "Send milk to the starving in Calcutta," or "Quit work and read Plato," or even "Buy granny a new rocker." In fact the answers were as follows: buy a house, live it up, save some money, buy property, take a holiday, buy stocks, start a business, and "other." The answer "other" may have been other-wordly but only 6 per cent offered it. Given more money, Canadians say they would invest it or spend it.

Another Gallup Poll asked Canadians what the country's major problems were – inflation (57 per cent), unemployment (8 per cent), energy (7 per cent), government (5 per cent), unions (3 per cent), pollution (3 per cent), US domination (2 per cent), other (10 per cent) and can't say (3 per cent). Now perhaps a few of the "others" and "can't says" said or thought that the real trouble was that Canadians had more money than was

17

good for them, that it was a damn shame and a stop should be put to it. *Perhaps* but we may be forgiven if we doubt it.

What emerges from these polls, as I look at them, is that there are no rich Canadians. Instead the menace of inflation is creating huge new classes of deprivation. A columnist in a major Canadian paper wrote recently about the "middle and upper-middle class poor," what we might call the rich-poor. These are the people who want and expect to own a comfortable home but who resent having to consign themselves to perpetual servitude in order to pay for it. These are the ex steak-eaters who now survive on hamburger from Monday to Friday. These are the people who formerly traded their big cars every few years but who now nurse anxiously the quietly rusting piles of steel. More tragically these are the people who saved for their retirements only to find that it is their savings which have retired – into oblivion.

The system demands consumption

The idea that Canadians do not consider themselves rich may have traces of irony, but in fact it is most serious. This country and its people have undergone the incredible transformation of the industrial revolution, the cybernetic revolution, and the information revolution to emerge from the other end as a "post-industrial society." We have undergone mass production and mass consumption to emerge as the "affluent society." And yet, as a people, as individuals, we are still terribly insecure.

Out of the fantastic economic growth of the last century, accelerated in the past twenty-five years, you might have guessed that a kind of economic cushion would have been created, permitting us to relax our demands. But just the opposite seems to be happening. The inflation of the 1970s has generated bitter competition among all groups and sectors, some trying to keep up, others trying to gain. Those facing hardship, in their own minds at least, are not only the low income groups but professionals like teachers and civil servants and, incredibly, doctors. The search for material security is a never-ending one.

The conclusion is a sombre one. As material prosperity grows we do not need less, we need more. How can this be? The answer, very simply, is that economic growth not only satisfies old demands, it also creates new ones. Economic development is only partly a rational, carefully calculated provision of our basic requirements. It is also an ever-widening circle of demands, wants, and hopes all of which gradually, over time are transformed into needs.

The point can be illustrated in many ways but a few examples follow. In our grandparents' day the automobile was first a foolish and monstrous contraption and then a status-bearing luxury. Fifty years later, the car is a plain necessity in the eyes of most North Americans, though still a status-symbol for some and increasingly a foolish and monstrous contraption for others.

In short *need* is not something which the stomach forces upon us. It is something learned, like the alphabet or chasing girls. And we are always learning. Twenty years ago the dishwasher was a luxury. Today it is in that twilight zone between luxury and necessity, soon to join refrigerators and stoves and vacuum cleaners in the arsenal of human needs.

For many of our parents owning their own home was a lifetime dream to be planned and saved for. For the children raised in those homes it is the "standard of living," the normal material condition rather than a dream. The examples of this type of economic history are endless: the striving of one generation becoming the common inheritance of the next, taken for granted but the loss a traumatic thing.

This is not just the story of individual aspiration. Our society is geared to it, our politics founded upon it. The collective ideals which motivate many of us are essentially material in nature – a beautiful home, secure and rising income, exciting vacations, and more of the same for our children. These ideals generate images – with the considerable aid of the advertising industry – against which almost any man's holdings seem shabby in comparison. The "typical" home in *Canadian Homes and Gardens* is an untypical $200,000 mansion.

And the refrain of politics must necessarily be growth. The government that fails to produce growth – or has the misfortune to be in office when it fails to occur – is in big trouble. The economy must generate more jobs at higher incomes or the system itself will collapse. Thus the demand for more is a never-ending demand – or so it seems – and reaches into every nook and cranny of our society.

And why not? Surely every goal in life – power, knowledge, wealth – is an inexhaustible one. Why should wealth be any different? Why should there be any upper limit on the material ambitions of Canadians? After all we are a long way from the ideal of a Caddy in every garage. The material ideal is a beautiful one, the most beautiful one, for millions of people, not only Canadians. Why should it be abandoned at some point arbitrarily called "enough"?

Because there are limits. Because the stuff out of which wealth flows is limited. Because there are many others whose needs are so much greater than our needs.

Canadians are finally recognizing that there are limits to the demands we can make on the economy without courting disaster. The wage-and-price control system imposed by the federal government is formal recognition of the need for restraint. But the need for limits extends far beyond domestic financial concerns. There are limits to the amount of injustice that people can stand; there are limits to how much exploitation the planet can stand. But this devouring of resources to satisfy our infinite invention of needs takes place while hundreds of millions of people are engaged in the more primitive task of seeking enough to eat – enough to stay alive.

But of course saying this changes nothing. We have known for a very long time that others were desperately poor while we were only "poorer than we would like to be." This realization has had very slight effect on our desire and determination to get more and our success in so doing. The reason for this is that most Canadians have regarded the great poverty of others, no matter how unfortunate, as essentially unrelated to our pursuit of wealth. It is now obvious that this belief is false.

As a rich country in a poor world, do we Canadians really care about the global human condition? Or should we, in honesty, accept the charges that we are smug, selfish, and indifferent?

This is a question we'd better start facing up to because it's clear to me that we're more concerned with higher gas prices for our cars than attacking the reasons for the hungry bellies of the world.

Chapter 2

One Billion People . . . Struggling to Survive

The global village is not a pretty village. True, there are some very comfortable neighbourhoods with tree-lined streets and spacious houses. But the slums impress the visitor. Shacks. Dirt. Stink. Children with bloated bellies and eyes of fear. Men and women shuffling in drudgery. And, strangely, some islands of affluence right in the poorest areas.

Marshall McLuhan gave us this metaphor – the global village – to describe the effect of technology and communications in shrinking the distances between peoples whose great differences in cultures, languages, colours, and religions have historically contributed to so much ignorance of one another.

The global village is a dangerous cliché. It lulls us into the delusion that there is the same unity and harmony of life world-wide that we associate with the villages we know. The modern world is not harmonized; it is fractured. There is no peace of mind because there is a war of the spirit. The rich minority are getting richer at the expense of the poor majority. The rhetoric of the global village is shattered by the millions of hungry, sick, penniless, and dispossessed. Their daily life makes a mockery of the slogan, "human dignity."

No, the world is not one. It is made up of four main parts.

Only by examining these four worlds can we understand the profound changes in international relationships that we must cope with.

The *First World* comprises the industrial democracies, mostly in the West. The United States and Canada, of course, belong to this world, along with Western Europe. So do Australia, New Zealand, and Japan. The total population is 662 million and the birth rate is low. The per capita GNP (the gross national product divided by the number of people) is $3,720 and rising.*

The *Second World* is made up of the Communist states, led by the U.S.S.R. and China and including a string of East European states, Cuba, and North and South Vietnam. China considers itself a Third World country because it identifies itself with the struggle of these countries. But it is included in this classification because it has a centrally-planned economy, the characteristic of Communist states. Total population is 1.2 billion. Per capita GNP: $1,049.

The *Third World* is the term commonly used for the developing countries, but because of the upheavals caused by the quintupling of energy prices, these countries now have to be divided into two classes. Nearly seventy countries make up the Third World in this classification. They comprise most of Latin America, the Middle East, and some parts of Asia and Africa. Some countries, such as Saudi Arabia, Kuwait, Venezuela, Nigeria, Indonesia, and Algeria have new-found wealth in oil exports. Others, like Ghana, Mexico, South Korea, and Uruguay are in various stages of development. Taken as a whole, they are far below the material standard of the First World, but they have made some progress toward improved living standards. Total population is 903 million and the birth rate is high. Per capita GNP: $784.

The *Fourth World* is a relatively new term but essential to describe the thirty-five countries most severely affected by the international economic upheaval of the mid-seventies. Short of

* The figures here are 1974 estimates. (See Tables, pp. 122-126).

food, energy, and fertilizer and trying to cope with the highest population growth rate in the world, they can only be regarded as economic hardship cases. They include India, Bangladesh, Pakistan, Burma, Ethiopia, Zaire, Tanzania. All told, their estimated 1974 population was 942 million and the total now exceeds one billion. Per capita GNP: $149.

Most of the developing countries of the Third and Fourth Worlds are caught up in a critical situation. The consequences of the continuing world-wide inflation, the sudden surge in the cost of oil, the deterioration in their terms of trade, and the prolonged recession in their export markets have combined to endanger their economic future. The net effect of these external forces has been to reduce their prospective rates of economic growth, and to increase their foreign exchange requirements.

But it is the Fourth World, facing stagnation, that is now the focus of development concern. Robert McNamara, president of the World Bank, has sounded this warning: "It is the very poorest countries, countries that collectively contain a billion human beings, which face the bleakest prospects – the prospects of virtually no increase at all in their desperately low per capita incomes for the rest of the decade. This stagnation does not mean inconvenience, or a minor sacrifice of comfort, or the simple postponement of a consumer satisfaction. It means struggling to survive at the very margin of life itself."

"One billion people . . . struggling to survive."
The delineation of this Fourth World is but the latest of the jolting shocks of the seventies. The global food, fertilizer, and fuel crises; galloping world-wide inflation; the population surge; new economic forces from transnational corporations to the breakdown of the dollar; the spread of nuclear power. This list forms just the outline of world conditions that the futurologist Alvin Toffler now describes as a state of "eco-spasm."

It is clear that we have crossed the frontier into a new era of global life. But our systems – both personal and national – are reacting against this accelerating journey because we do not have an assurance of survival. We have neither equipment nor answers.

The problems of energy, capitalization, and pollution are transnational but we do not have a transnational body to enforce solutions. The air is filled with the soothing word "detente," which should relax East-West tensions, but Solzhenitsyn warns the West that Communist ideology still aims to destroy our society. We have had twenty-five years of foreign aid and now we learn that development conditions are worse than ever.

No matter how unsettling the age of eco-spasm is to us, it remains a fact that the task of meeting basic human needs is now the centrepiece of international politics.

Put in a nutshell, the situation is this:

The First World has excellent prospects for pulling out of recession and accruing even more wealth (added to its towering standard of living).

The Second World, dominated by Russia and China, is not active in the problems of world trade and development, beyond rhetorical blasts at the West. The Russians have become rich and strong. The Chinese experience of self-reliance is attracting a great deal of interest because it suggests that even the most monumental problems, involving the lives of hundreds of millions of people, may be capable of solution where will, commitment, and resources are applied.

The Third World, struggling against time and the vicissitudes of world prices, is showing some development progress – with progress being defined as basic human needs.

The Fourth World is mired in deprivation.

And so the principal social issue in the world today is whether the developed world will make a greater effort to help save the developing world from suffering and hopelessness which statistics cannot convey. "All that is required to assist these peoples so immensely less privileged," says McNamara, "is a simple willingness to dedicate a tiny percentage of the additional wealth that will accrue to the developed nations over the next five years."

Concentration of economic power

In order to understand the reasons for such economic disparity we have to examine why three-quarters of the world's income, investment, services, and almost all the world's research are in the hands of one-quarter of its people. We will then begin to see the consequences of almost five centuries of colonial control which concentrated economic power so overwhelmingly in the hands of a small group of nations.

The international systems of commerce set up during and after World War II perpetuated the economic strength of those who were already strong. Indeed, an extraordinary world economic expansion followed the Agreements of Bretton Woods (1944), and the General Agreement on Tariffs and Trade (GATT) which were designed to provide open and expanding trade, free movement of investment capital and technology, readily available supplies of raw materials, and international cooperation. It was supposed that the increasing wealth of the rich would then trickle down to the poor of the earth.

The economic order established in the post-war years served some nations well, says Shridath S. Ramphal, secretary-general of the Commonwealth, "but it is indisputably the case that it has served many countries ill; among these are the countries that it has helped to make the countries of the Third World."

The political liberation that swept through Asia and Africa created a host of nation states; these new states soon found themselves confronted with tariff systems they could not cope with. The tariff system with low tariffs for raw materials and high tariffs for industrial products blocked the industrialization of the poor countries. They received low prices for the export of their primary commodities while having to pay increasingly higher prices to import manufactured goods from the industrialized nations. The capital creation and credit systems remained firmly in the hands of the United States and Europe. While diversified aid programs were set up to help the developing nations they had the principal effect of perpetuating their dependency on the rich nations.

Pre-emption by the rich of a disproportionate share of key resources conflicted directly with longer term interests of the poor by impairing their ultimate access to resources necessary to their development and by increasing their cost. In fact, the very cheapness of the materials imported from the developing countries was one element encouraging the industrialized nations to indulge in careless and extravagant use. Oil at just over a dollar a barrel in the early post-war years stimulated a growth in energy use of between 6 and 11 per cent a year in the West.

The people of the Western countries were seemingly oblivious to the crushing effect we had on the world economy – and any concern we expressed was directed at the poor for having too many babies. There was almost no recognition that the world population problem has a double thrust: rapidly expanding numbers of people in the developing regions of the world, and the high standard of living in the developed regions.

Underdevelopment causes population growth

Medical and health advances have cut mortality rates at both ends of life; more babies survive and people live longer. Nearly half the population of the world is under the age of fifteen. There are now twice as many potential mothers alive as a generation ago. Even with declining fertility rates, world population will not level off until late into the next century at the earliest.

It took from mankind's first evolution until about 1800 to reach the one billion mark. We reached two billion in 1928, three billion in 1961, and four billion in 1975. Thus the intervals for accommodating an additional billion human beings have fallen from 128 to 33 to 14 years. The time span is continuing to shrink. Demographers can now say with certainty that there will be seven billion people by the year 2000. Another world on top of this, doubling the demands and hopes of today.

The cumulative effect and uneven distribution of this growth, averaging 2 per cent a year, makes it extremely serious. Most of this increase is taking place in the developing world, which already contains two-thirds of humanity. When the double phenomena of population growth and urbanization are considered, "eco-catastrophe," as Maurice Strong, a former Director of the UN Environmental Programme describes it, is certain. The mounting demands of urban populations, swollen by the influx of desperate migrants from rural areas, already overwhelm our ability to provide basic services like water, sewage, schools, and hospitals. Slums, shanty towns, and squatter settlements will become ever more prevalent over the face of the earth, as symbols of organized society's failure to provide adequate habitation for people. "It is not squatters that are obscene," McNamara says. "It is the economic circumstances that make squatter settlements necessary that are obscene."

Our understanding of the total population problem is incomplete if we do not grasp the full import of one-third of humanity consuming two-thirds of the earth's wealth and resources. A baby born in Canada, where the population problem is not visible, will grow up consuming fifty times the resources and energy that a baby in the heavily-populated developing regions will consume. This implies that the developed world is responsible for a much greater per capita environment impact than less-developed nations which naturally view this as exploitative.

Therefore, the problem in the Third and Fourth Worlds is not population as such. Rather it is extreme poverty perpetuated by the control which the developed world exercises over the bulk of the earth's wealth and resources. In taking for granted ever higher standards of living, which put such strain on the resource and environment capacities of the planet, the minority of rich countries get richer at the expense of the multiplying poor. Considering all these factors, the World Population Conference in Bucharest in 1974 emphasized that large populations are not the cause of underdevelopment but the result of underdevelopment.

India, whose teeming masses are often photographed by the Western media to illustrate the "population crisis," has expanded birth control clinics through the country for the past two decades. The results have been marginal and the country now takes the official view that fertility levels can be effectively lowered only if family planning becomes an integral part of a broader development strategy. "Our experience has conclusively shown that purely clinical approaches are not enough to effectively influence the general fertility levels," India's spokesman declared at Bucharest.

In the developing countries, couples still want many children because they fear that several may die, and they need children to work and help support them as they grow old. Often, as couples become aware of the fact that many more of their offspring survive than did those of their own parents, they want to give birth to fewer children, but may not know how. Many women then turn to abortion which, tragically, has become a widely used method of family limitation today.

The World Population Plan puts family planning in this context:
– Encourage appropriate education concerning responsible parenthood and make available to persons who so desire advice and means of achieving it.
– Respect and ensure, regardless of their overall demographic goals, the right of persons to determine, in a free, informed, and responsible manner, the number and spacing of their children. In other words, the freedom of each couple to make its own determination is to be preserved while at the same time family planning information is to be made available. The Bucharest Conference put this approach in the context of respect for human life, maintenance of the family as the basic unit of society, and the right of women to equal participation in educational, social, economic, cultural, and political life.

What India and many other developing countries are telling the world is that because poverty is the main cause of the massive increase in population, it is poverty that must be eradicated. Then will follow a sharp decline in the rate of population growth. In the developed countries, population stability has followed economic development.

Family planning, when pushed by the West, can easily be construed by the Third World as a device to salve our consciences without adopting structural reform of world economic and social systems. Many countries told the World Population Conference that family planning was not a magic panacea. As a result, the World Population Plan of Action was rewritten to put a heavy emphasis on "rapid socio-economic development" rather than family planning as the route to population stability.

This shift of emphasis was most dramatically evidenced by John D. Rockefeller 3rd, for forty years one of the leading figures in the Planned Parenthood movement. "I have changed my mind," he said, in the face of mounting evidence that "family planning alone is not adequate" to curb population growth and improve the quality of people's lives.

Rockefeller, who is the founder and chairman of the Population Council, an international research agency, spoke deeply of his long experience.

"It turns out that women who avail themselves of family planning are chiefly those who already have had many children. Over the forty-year space I have referred to, the population of the world has increased by 86 per cent, from 2.1 billion to 3.9 billion. And the absolute number of people in poverty has continued to grow. Clearly, the programs that have been undertaken have proved inadequate when compared to the magnitude of the problems . . .

"The integration of population and development suggests development planning that will be creatively and fundamentally different than in the past. Clearly, development plans must be shaped within the realities of the world as it exists today . . . not in terms of 100 years ago. By this I mean that the classic model of development, originating in the Industrial Revolution, is no longer realistic.

"The development of a country today must have an overriding moral purpose – to improve the lives of all the people of the country. The need is to beat back poverty and hunger and disease, to provide more jobs, better education, improved health care."

The spokesman for India at Bucharest put this point cogently: "The best contraceptive is development."

A massive list of injustices

Some of these facts of global life only became apparent in the West following the collapse of the world monetary system in 1971. The next year, widespread harvest failures and a boom in demand brought food stocks perilously low even in normally surplus areas. Rapid inflation hit the economies of both developed and developing market economies, and the following year saw massive changes in relative prices. Oil went up 4.5 times in price from January 1973 to January 1974, wheat doubled in price in the same period. The prospect of continuing plenty was seriously questioned for the first time in three decades as an international recession combined with galloping inflation and serious imbalances in world trade and payments.

The net result of all this was to make a group of petroleum exporting nations (OPEC) a powerful new force on the world economic scene. OPEC shook up the West to the realization that the days of cheap energy were over; and OPEC welded together the developing nations (now called the Group of Seventy-Seven) in a combative stance against the West. The call for a new international economic order went up.

At first this sounded like more phrase-making. For a while the United Nations rang with charges and counter-charges, the inevitable expression of anger. But why would there not be anger in compiling a list of massive social injustice?
– According to the Food and Agriculture Organization (FAO) the world has never seen as many undernourished people as today; one billion suffer hunger or malnutrition.
– According to the World Health Organization (WHO) there have never been as many people without access to pure drinking water.
– According to the United Nations Educational, Scientific and

Cultural Organization (UNESCO) the world has never had as high a rate of adult illiteracy – half the world's population has never attended school.

– According to the International Labour Organization (ILO) the world has never had as many unemployed and under-employed people as today.

Specific examples of world wide economic injustice would themselves fill a book. Here are but three:

1. Bananas in Latin America. Several Latin American countries which depend to a large extent for their foreign exchange earnings on the sale of bananas have seen the price of bananas fall about 30 per cent in the past twenty years. Producer countries have been able to do little to reverse the decline in price since the banana industry is controlled by three large US transnational corporations (United Brands, Castle and Cook, Inc., and Del Monte).

According to the United Nations Conference on Trade and Development (UNCTAD) these three corporations control the transportation, shipping, insuring, ripening, wholesaling, and retailing of the six-million ton world trade in bananas, the most important year-round fresh fruit. From 1960 to the early 1970s, the quantity of bananas exported rose substantially but the value increased only 1 per cent. And their *actual value* decreased because the developing countries had to pay a great deal more to import manufactured goods from developed countries. In 1960 a tractor cost the equivalent value of three tons of bananas, and in 1970 the same tractor cost eleven tons of bananas. No wonder the banana exporters are trying to put teeth into a producers' association.

2. Jute in Asia. Bangladesh relies on jute and jute fabrics like sacks and carpet-bagging for almost half its foreign earnings which are needed to import vital commodities, such as food and petroleum. Now the jute industry faces severe competition from synthetic fibres like polypropylene resin, made in the developed countries. The demand for jute is falling, the tariff barriers are high, and the result is that Bangladesh is driven further into debt.

This situation is not peculiar to Bangladesh. Three-quarters of the developing world's export earnings come from raw materials. And most of them are dependent on demand from the rich world, are subject to import restrictions, and are coming under increasing pressure from synthetic substitutes made possible by the high degree of technology in the West.

3. Firewood in Africa. In Upper Volta, virtually all trees within forty-three miles of Ouagadougou have been cut down and used as fuel for cooking and heating. This was the finding of a researcher for the Worldwatch Institute, which warns that the intensifying shortage of firewood represents a special kind of energy crisis that could lead to "the most profound ecological challenge of the late twentieth century."

The growing demand for firewood is causing such widespread deforestation that subsequent erosion and loss of fertility are rendering huge tracts of land useless for food production. In many parts of Sahelian Africa, woodcutters have removed enough trees to speed up the advance of the Sahara.

Whether the story is told in books, reams of statistics, or film documentaries, the same picture emerges: a "permanent emergency" exists for a quarter of humanity living in the Fourth World who do not have enough food, medicine, shelter, schools, or job opportunities.

The cities of developing countries continue to grow by millions without any corresponding growth in employment or resources. In the past, people were attracted by the cities whereas today they are only repelled by the countryside. Food supply grows more rapidly than ever before but population grows faster. In short, the inertia of underdevelopment is enormous, far greater than we expected.

Development involves costs that were not previously anticipated. The Green Revolution helped modernize agricultural production but it did so by vastly increasing the need for more science, more technology, more fertilizer, more oil and, as always, more money. So Bangladesh produces more food than it ever has but is more dependent on outside resources. Education is another example. Most countries placed this near the top of their list of priorities only to discover that there are more graduates than there are jobs. Development not only satisfies human demand, it creates it as well.

And then there is the failure of justice. If you mention development to the average person he thinks of helping the poor. Despite the considerable growth in GNP in some developing countries the resulting wealth has not reached the poor to any significant degree.

To take only three examples: During the past decade *Brazil's* GNP in real terms grew by 2.5 per cent per year. Yet the share of the national income received by the poorest 40 per cent of the population declined from 10 per cent in 1960 to 8 per cent in 1970.

Kenya, a Fourth World country, has four main sources of wealth: land, tourism, commerce, and wildlife. Each, reports the *Times of London*, has been grabbed up by the relatives of President Jomo Kenyatta. Known in Kenya simply as the Royal Family, this private syndicate operates with a mixture of aggressive business tactics and unabashed use of the powers of the state in maintaining control over the wealth of Kenya.

Between 1950 and 1969 *Mexico's* income per capita grew, in real terms, by 3 per cent per year. But the richest 10 per cent of the population received about half of the total national income at the beginning of the period and an even larger share at the end. The share of the poorest 20 per cent during the same period sank from 6 per cent to 4 per cent.

The same failure of justice characterizes the international scene. A principal objective of development was to close the gap between rich nations and poor. Twenty-five years later, the gap is greater than ever before and growing rapidly.

The "trickle down" theory has been exploded. The poor are

not benefiting proportionately from the gains of the rich. They have felt most severely the impact of food shortages and higher food prices. They have faced rising costs for petroleum and a sharp jump in the cost of fertilizer. The extra cost of oil imports alone in 1974, estimated at $10 billion, more than wiped out all the aid developing countries received the previous year. We will return later to the vagaries of the international aid program, but for the moment let us note that the purchasing power of the developing countries is declining, not increasing (the World Bank estimated a $14 billion drop in 1975 compared with the level of the early 1970s). The OPEC countries are providing five times more aid to the Fourth World than the developed world, but even this help does not remove the core of the problem.

No shortage of food

The problem is not one of absolute physical shortage but of economic and social maldistribution and misuse. The food, fertilizer and energy crises illustrate this.

In the face of famine and malnourishment, plenty of grain exists. But it is being eaten in the First and Second Worlds by very well-fed people. Grain consumption in North America has grown by 350 pounds per capita, largely in meat products, since 1965, to reach 1,900 pounds today. Yet this extra 350 pounds is almost equal to an Indian's total annual consumption. North Americans were hardly starving in 1965. The increase since then has contributed to super-consumption which even threatens health.

Meanwhile, in the poor world, studies have shown that there are 300 million children who are physically or mentally retarded by malnutrition – and this is in addition to the 15 million who die each year from malnutrition and related diseases. It requires only a small release from the "surplus" of the rich to meet the global shortfall in food. There could hardly be a more vivid example of the overconsumption of the wealthy nations contributing directly to the underconsumption of the world's poor.

Two British film-makers, Alan Hart and Ian McFarlane, trekked through twenty countries for two years to produce a vibrant documentary on development entitled *Five Minutes to Midnight*. The film graphically shows the disparity in consumption between the rich and poor worlds in a way that reaches the heart of the development question.

We see Julius Nyerere, president of Tanzania in his study, immediately after several scenes of gaudy consumption in the West. "In the rich world," Nyerere says, "people think if you have more and more of material goods you become more and more of a human being." He cannot repress a chuckle at this absurdity. "Until you change that situation the rich world has no means of helping the poor world because they don't have enough to fulfil the ambitions they set for themselves – which is the possession of material wealth."

PART TWO: THE WAY THINGS OUGHT TO BE

Chapter 3

Development Means Human Solidarity

I often think of Bishop Peter Sarpong of Ghana whom I met at an international conference on development. A big, black man with serious eyes and a relieving smile, he can articulate the concerns of the Third and Fourth Worlds with passion and clarity. "You must stop thinking of us in Black Africa as underdeveloped," he would thunder. "We are developed. What we want is liberation." These words usually take on a special meaning for me when I am caught in one of the interminable traffic jams of New York or Toronto or the other super-cities that are supposed to be the reflection of what development can achieve.

Are the Third and Fourth Worlds less developed because they do not have the technological benefits that we enjoy? Is Canada more developed because our gross national product is so much bigger? Does development consist of giving aid to people who are not as productive as we are?

Asking these kinds of questions is the first essential step in comprehending the reason why things are the way they are. Yes, the developing world needs bread, but merely to stand on the street corner and hand out bread to the hungry or even to build a bigger and better bakery does not get to the core of the problem. Inevitably we are driven back to the fundamental question: What is development?

Only when we grasp the relationship of every human being to the economic and social processes can we then adequately respond to the crisis of our time. Despite the headlines of the day, the crisis our civilization faces is not one of energy or food production or population, it is a crisis of humanity itself. Our expression of concern for the Third and Fourth Worlds is nothing short of fraudulent unless we acknowledge that we have become "over-developed" at the expense of the "under-developed." This is not just history or moralizing or playing psychiatrist; it is a hard-headed recognition that the industrialized societies thrive today by continuing to place obstacles in the path of developing people without most of us even knowing what we are doing.

That is why we must understand the meaning of the stirring photo of the earth brought back by the astronauts. There it shines as no earth dweller had ever seen it before: blue, flecked with white cloud patterns, a beautiful small globe set against the black void of space through which it is whirling at incredible speed. Spaceship Earth, Barbara Ward has called it, a unique space vehicle, providing a viable eco-system for human beings, but with quite limited resources. The fundamental lesson of the photo is the oneness of our humanity on earth – a oneness that must triumph over the artificial division of the world into four parts.

Only by examining the whole world as a community bonded by our common humanity can we then understand what development should entail. This brings us directly to the key question of the value of each human being. For if we do not remember what it is that makes a human being human it is all too easy to submerge the dignity and rights of the individual in the name of progress.

This approach is equally productive whether we are a Christian putting our faith in the gospel of Jesus; a Jewish believer in *Mitzvah*, the divine commandment to alleviate poverty and restore the image of the divine in every man; or a secularist who perceives that the harmony of creation has been broken. People of diverse religious outlooks can converge on the same practical principles and conclusions provided that they similarly revere, perhaps for quite different reasons, truth and intelligence, human dignity, freedom, brotherly love, and the absolute value of moral good.

According to the almost unanimous opinion of believers and unbelievers alike, all things on earth should be related to the human person as their centre and crown. But what do we mean precisely when we speak of the human person? The philosopher Jacques Maritain offers this description:

"We do not mean merely that he is an individual, in the sense that an atom, a blade of grass, a fly or an elephant is an individual. Man is an individual who holds himself in hand by intelligence and will. He does not exist only in a physical manner. He has a spiritual superexistence through knowledge and love; he is, in a way, a universe in himself, a microcosm, in which the great universe in its entirety can be encompassed through knowledge; and through love, he can give himself completely to beings who are to him, as it were, other selves, a relation for which no equivalent can be found in the physical world. The human person possesses these characteristics because in the last analysis, man, this flesh and these perishable bones which are animated and activated by a divine fire, exists 'from the womb to the tomb' by virtue of the very existence of his soul, which dominates time and death. Spirit is the root of personality. The notion of personality thus involves that of totality and independence; no matter how poor and crushed he may be, a person, as such, is a whole and subsists in an independent manner."[1]

The individual and the community

This description of humanity provides the framework for development. For true development is not about things but about the

[1] *Principes d'une politique humaniste*, (Paris: Paul Hartmann, 1945), pp. 15-16.

whole person. Development includes the passage from misery toward the possession of necessities, but it also means victory over social scourges, the growth of knowledge, and the acquisition of culture.

The Dag Hammarskjöld Foundation, which has studied these questions intensively, summed up this point: "Development is a whole; it is an integral, value-loaded, cultural process; it encompasses the natural environment, social relations, education, production, consumption and well-being." There is hope for peace and justice only if we develop a world community characterized by what Maritain has called "integral humanism."

Development therefore requires a political, social and economic order that will affirm and develop the dignity proper to every person. This is the proper meaning of human liberation, and this is why the political liberation achieved by most of the developing world since World War II has been followed by demands for economic liberation too, as my friend, Bishop Sarpong insists upon.

A liberated person is one who has the economic basis and political freedom to develop his true potential as a human person in keeping with the common good. Each person must be allowed to discover his true self and express his own authenticity. The liberation of the human being, then, does indeed have a deeper dimension than economic but without access to food, shelter, education, employment, and health care there can be no liberation.

We can see now why we must redefine the purpose of development to include the concept of the whole person. Any process of growth that does not lead to the fulfilment of the basic needs of food, shelter, education, employment, and health care – or even worse, disrupts them – is a travesty of the idea of development. Just as poverty is destructive of the well-being of man, superabundance and the satisfaction of endless wants is destructive.

Obviously, at a time when the gap between rich and poor is

widening, the world community must give primary attention to the economic base of development. We are still in a stage where the most important concern of development is the level of satisfaction of basic needs for the poorest sections in each society which can be as high as 40 per cent of the population.

The primary purpose of economic growth, then, should be to ensure the improvement of conditions for these groups. A growth process that benefits only the wealthiest minority and maintains or even increases the disparities between and within countries is not development. It is exploitation. The experience of a quarter of a century shows us that the "trickle down" theory, in which the poor are better off as the rich get richer is illusory. We must therefore reject the comforting posture of growth for us first, justice in the distribution of benefits later.

The satisfaction of basic needs opens the way to those other values and goals of development: freedom of expression, the right to give and receive ideas and stimulus, the right to find self-realization in work, the right not to be exploited as another tool in the hands of the employer. There is, finally a deep social need in people of all colours and cultures to participate in shaping the basis of their own existence, and to make some contribution to re-shaping the world's future.

We can now see, in this larger view of development, that the idea that the developing nations should become like us is ludicrous. For just as it is wrong to debase development by having no floor for economic realization, it is equally wrong to treat the life support systems of the world as if there were no ceiling. And that is what we have done in the Western world.

In the search for models of human development, we ought to be very leery about putting ourselves forward. It is really arrogant to suggest that development is the effort to imitate the historical model of the countries which for various reasons happen to be rich today. This is what comes from interpreting history from the Western point of view. As the sociologists put it, ethnocentricity distorts our perspective.

The ideas of progress, creative growth, expansion, surpluses, inexhaustible resources have been synonymous with the development of Western man since the industrial revolution. Science and technology have been the driving forces behind us. This is true no matter whether people live under a capitalist or socialist system of government. Industrial civilization is predicated on expansion. When we are not growing, we are in trouble. Growth has thus become an end in itself.

Now, however, we are starting to realize that unlimited industrial production and economic expansion to satisfy an artificially stimulated consumer demand are a voracious trap for the industrialized nations.

Roadblocks in their way

In a later chapter, I will return to the subject of what individuals in our society can do to contribute to the development of an equitable social order. But now, in this overall consideration of what development is (and how we have overdone it) we must go on to consider the roadblocks we have placed in the way of the developing countries. Not only do we have the effrontery to consider the Third World "under-developed" when in fact it is rich in values and cultures, we have deliberately and systematically exploited them and prevented them from developing an adequate economic base.

The industrial rise of the West was directly linked with the success of colonialism which exploited raw materials and labour in the tropical countries; moreover, this very enterprise often halted developing systems in these countries and blocked their evolution.

Not long ago, I met a brilliant African exponent of this perspective, Ellen Johnson-Sirleaf, a thirty-seven-year-old Liberian who is a loan officer with the World Bank. A Harvard graduate in economic development, she was formerly assistant minister of finance in Liberia. Tall and a bit aloof, Ms. Johnson-Sirleaf conveys determination and cold anger as she recounts how Africa's automomy succumbed to the expansionist urges of the West. Africa, she points out, has a heritage of values derived from indigenous civilizations thousands of years old, "but it is the vicissitudes of history which have transmuted, corrupted and reshaped her original geographic, ethnic and cultural endowments."

Egypt was the cradle of civilization for ten thousand years when the rest of the world wallowed in barbarism. Relatively sophisticated agricultural and engineering systems operated in the Nile area. Gradually, her people spread out and the Negroes of South Sahara Africa developed with an abundance of resources. Their societies were mostly of the communal type, based on the clan or extended family with common ownership of land. Ms. Johnson-Sirleaf concluded:

"Thus Black Africa directed her energies toward developing social and political structures, such as the famed ancient Kingdoms of Dahomey, Benie, Songhai, and Mali, and toward systems of morality and ethics rather than toward scientific and material pursuits. It was in this state of civilization that the first modern encounter with Europe occurred."

From the fifteenth century onward, the gathering forces of explorers and traders intruded further inland in Black Africa which lacked the capacity to resist. Soon the trading posts of Portugal, France, Britain, and Holland became foreign annexations attained through armed might, and it then became an easy step to reduce Africa to the function of supplying labour for the homelands of Europe and America.

During the next three centuries (1500 – 1800) European nations scrambled for their pieces of African territory, carving the continent into heterogeneous groupings without respect to language, history, customs, or physical characteristics. By the time the 1885 Berlin Conference completed the pillage, the Egyptian civilization was lost in the ruins of antiquity, the victim of mercantile man's lust for ivory, gold, cotton, and copper.

The colonization of Africa is frequently presented as an humanitarian effort, a messianic effort to Christianize and develop the African barbarian. Undoubtedly, some of what was done was well intentioned and conferred lasting benefit. But more was done for selfish reasons, in a brutal way and with evil consequences. In either case everything was done on such a massive scale and so suddenly that it thoroughly disrupted and disoriented these societies so that their own capacities for managing development were eroded.

Africa is by no means the only example of ruthless mercantilism halting what would have been a natural growth. In India, for example, at the beginning of the nineteenth century, a flourishing textile industry arose in Calcutta. But the British imposed a commercial monopoly and the Indian textile industry virtually disappeared. It is a fiction to think that it was cultural obstacles that prevented industrial expansion from occurring. Today India is the tenth industrial nation of the world, and this has largely been accomplished since her independence.

Ceylon offers another example. Irrigation projects to intensify the cultivation of rice were common there three centuries before Christ. Over the centuries tens of thousands of reservoirs and canals were built. "The overall picture of these works," says the Belgian sociologist Francois Houtart, "is impressive and demonstrates a remarkable degree of technical mastery. This method of production was the model for the entire social organization of these societies."

But with the arrival of the establishment of coffee and tea plantations, peasants were driven from their small landholdings. The irrigation system fell into disrepair (coffee and tea requiring less water) and rice production diminished rapidly. Ceylon became a rice importer and at the time of independence in 1948 Ceylon (now called Sri Lanka) had to import two-thirds of its food. Despite immense agricultural potential, she still is not self-sufficient and must spend valuable foreign currency for food importation instead of buying the equipment for economic development. Meanwhile, the coffee and tea plantations had made fortunes for the colonizers. The destruction of the agricultural economy of the Ceylonese was of small weight in the economic calculations of the British.

As we look at the modern era which began with the rush to

political liberation of the Third World following World War II, we must understand that economic domination has persisted and is the principal reason why millions upon millions of people cannot achieve self-reliance. There have indeed been immense aid projects, but in many ways the aid is a camouflage for the continuing practice of the small number of industrialized nations concentrating in their hands not only technology and wealth but the control of international mechanisms.

Again, this has been a common pattern throughout the Third World. The obstacles to economic development remain many: investments made by transnational companies with the aim of making a profit and not of developing a given population; the repatriation of profits from economically weak countries; price-fixing on the international market; the virtual Western monopoly of financial services and transport; withdrawing or withholding credits; embargoes; economic sanctions; the subversive use of intelligence agencies; repression including torture, counter-insurgency operations, and even full-scale intervention. The methods used to perpetuate this domination probably seem as "realistic" to the international power structure today as aggressive pioneering tactics did to the colonizers.

The elites of the poor societies
When the negative influence of the elites of the poor societies is added to all of the above obstacles, the goal of human development looks even further away.

What has happened is that, imitating the aggressiveness and acquisitiveness of the masters they fought to replace, the elite of the developing countries have built their own social structures that guarantee the first economic rewards for themselves at the expense of their own people. It would be the final hypocrisy in the name of development for the Third World managers and bureaucrats to enrich themselves by reproducing the pattern of Western industrialization while leaving it to the destitute majority to preserve the pre-existing cultures and traditional practices of history.

What development there has been in some Third and Fourth

World countries has mostly left the masses of people as poor as they had been. And, as we know, the poverty-stricken part of the total population has been increasing in many countries. Reforms aimed at improving the lot of the poor have either not been implemented or they have tended to aid the small upper class. "This is related," says Gunnar Myrdal, the Nobel Prize-winning economist, "to the fact that, despite their written constitutions, power belongs to an elite who embrace egalitarian ideals but in practice mostly look to what they conceive of as their own interests."

Myrdal believes that well-planned reforms to improve living levels of the poor can be productive by raising the quality of the labour force which in turn produces agriculture and health improvements. The very low productivity of man and land is a main cause of poverty in general, and undernourishment of the masses. Thus, he says, "we must conceive of development as the movement forward of an entire social system which includes, in addition to economic factors, all non-economic factors. There is a kind of circular causation, implying that if one condition changes, others will change in response."

A better distribution of land ownership throughout the developing world is an obvious essential. The present concentration of land ownership in the hands of the wealthy is a self-serving device that blocks internal development. Also, some poor countries seriously burden their budgets with disproportionate expenditures for armaments or for construction of prestige buildings, thus depriving their rural populations especially of fundamental goods.

Summing up this outline of true development and the continuing obstacles to it, we can see that it is impossible to expect the people of the Third and Fourth Worlds to become self-reliant while they are dominated by external and internal systems that perpetuate economic dependence.

Towards a harmonized, cooperative world
"The ideal we need," says the Cocoyoc Declaration, adopted at a UN Conference in 1974, "is a harmonized cooperative

world in which each part is a centre, living at the expense of nobody else, in partnership with nature and in solidarity with future generations." It remains to be seen whether ways of life and social systems can be evolved that are more just, less arrogant in their material demands, more respectful of the whole planetary environment – or whether the international power structure will continue to resist moves in this direction.

Let there be no mistake: this total concept of development I have been describing cannot be pursued, as the Dag Hammarskjöld Foundation insists, "without a radical modification of existing trends."

No system of development today is without serious defects. The capitalist countries are strong on production and political liberties but permit too great extremes in economic benefits; the socialist countries limit the economic gap but at the expense of both production and political liberties.

The economically developed societies, through the ceaseless pressure on resources, are pushing the "outer limits" of the planet's capacity. The economically underdeveloped societies cannot meet the "inner limit" of satisfying fundamental human needs.

The search for new models of development will prove fruitless unless we take into account universal principles such as social justice and the common good. Neither East nor West, mystics nor pragmatists, rich nor poor, Washington nor Moscow, old nor young has a monopoly on development, for it is multi-dimensional. Enlightenment will come from many sources – the spiritual-cultural traditions of the East and South as well as the economic-political achievements of the West and North. To be blunt, we must learn to know and respect our neighbour, remembering the extension of the neighbourhood in the global village.

Chapter 4

Progress Towards a New Economic Order

It was 4:00 a.m. when I walked out of the United Nations building into the pre-dawn stillness of midtown New York. The Seventh Special Session of the General Assembly had just passed a consensus document on international development, the result of around-the-clock negotiations between the developed and developing countries.

I was both exhilarated and exhausted as I looked around for a cab. The two-week Special Session was supposed to have concluded the previous Friday. Here it was Tuesday morning. The whole weekend had seen pressure mount almost to the bursting point. Could both sides agree on ways to start implementing a new economic order? Or would the spirit of good will evaporate when the bargaining got tough?

I felt as if I had been watching the world's biggest poker game, with all the bluffing, calling, and raising of stakes that stretch tempers in a casino. A bystander might have thought the chips were money, power, resources, oil – the big things that countries fight over. But on close inspection, the chips in my eyes were people – one billion of them who live a life of suffering because they do not have enough food, shelter, medicine, education, or jobs.

The Special Session was composed of speeches, great ideas, and what appeared to be a new spirit of harmony – as if everyone were finally convinced of the urgency of closing the rich-poor gap in the world. But it was when negotiations started on a draft document, prepared by the developing nations (the Group of Seventy-Seven), expressing what the rich world should actually do to meet the demands of the poor world that the poker players emerged.

I had gone to the session as a parliamentary observer, especially concerned with Canada's participation. As I went from meeting to meeting, I frequently felt intimidated, even submerged, by the negotiators and their card-playing ability. I kept asking myself what all this haggling over seemingly small points was actually doing to help the one billion people. Finally, as the weekend wore on, I became reconciled that there is no way around hard bargaining in the development picture. Humanism carries us only so far; and real changes are only made out of self-interest.

The global economic upheaval of the early-seventies confirmed for the developing countries that the existing economic system could no longer work in their interests. Those who had been following the development scene were already convinced that world poverty was the result of a complex and unjust economic system rather than the simple product of "backwardness." What was suddenly changing was the determination of the developing nations to band together for collective action. For years they had been pushed to the sidelines of international politics by the Cold War between East and West. Now the spectre of a different kind of war – over food, shelter, and opportunities – was on the horizon. Liberation movements in many countries rejected trickle-down development. Pushed from below, the developing countries began to push those above them.

In the midst of the economic crisis of 1972 – 75, the Organization of Petroleum Exporting Countries (OPEC) struck. The precipitous rise in oil prices had negative effects in the short run on some developing countries but it had a more profound positive and long-term effect. For the action sharply altered the balance of power in the world markets, redistributing resources massively. Eleven countries (Algeria, Ecuador, Gabon, Indonesia, Iran, Iraq, Kuwait, Libyan Arab Republic, Nigeria, Saudi Arabia, and Venezuela) found themselves with a $100 billion a year surplus. The balance of power in oil shifted dramatically. The industrialized nations suddenly found themselves in the condition long familiar in the Third World – lack of control over vital economic decisions.

OPEC demonstrated the degree to which the world market system – which has continuously operated to increase the power and wealth of the rich and to maintain the relative deprivation of the poor – is rooted in political relationships. These relationships can undergo profound reversals and transformations.

While the energy transformation was taking place, the economic crisis brought with it inflation which largely wiped out the previous gains of development. After years of the Green Revolution, there was widespread starvation again. Balance of payments rose disastrously. A general feeling developed that economic and social development was sliding backward rather than moving forward. "In a sense," the UN's Cocoyoc Declaration said, "a new economic order is already struggling to be born. The crisis of the old system can also be the opportunity of the new."

The proposals of the new economic order
In this setting – reversals of the world economy and growing solidarity of the Third World – a set of proposals for reform known as the New International Economic Order was put before the United Nations. Its main features include:

1) *International trade*
Most developing countries depend heavily on the trading of their raw materials and commodities to finance their development. However few of them produce oil or other materials with

high prices in the international market. The prices of their exports – established during the colonial era – have tended to fluctuate wildly and over the long run to decline in value relative to the cost of manufactured goods from the rich countries. A key objective of the new order is to reverse this situation through an overall or "integrated" approach which includes:

– *Indexation* which is the linking of the prices of developing countries' exports to the prices of their imports. Thus as the latter rose, the former would rise automatically as well.

– *General Commodity Agreement* embracing a wide range of raw materials important to the Third and Fourth Worlds such as wheat, rice and sugar, coffee and tea, cotton, jute and rubber and copper, tin and bauxite. The objective here is to stabilize the prices of these essential products through such mechanisms as international buffer stocks and financial arrangements to build the stocks and compensate for losses.

– *Producers Associations* somewhat along the lines of OPEC. From the point of view of developing countries such associations would strengthen their bargaining power and help correct the historical injustice of low and erratic prices for commodity exports. As Jamaica's Prime Minister Michael Manley puts it in *Background to Issues of the Seventh General Session*, "the Third World has been driven by its poverty and the inexorable workings of the free trade system to the discovery of the producer association." There are two possibilities in the development of such associations. "They can either become the instruments through which nations conduct a rational dialogue with consumers within the framework of a New International Economic Order or for want of dialogue they will become increasingly the instruments through which the Third World takes such unilateral action as is demanded by the powers of survival and equity."

– *Reducing Tariffs*. In the past, multilateral trade negotiations within the framework of the General Agreement on Tariffs and Trade (GATT) have led to reductions in tariff barriers in successive "rounds." But these steps have primarily affected – and benefited – the developed market economy countries, *i.e.*, the rich. The developing countries want faster and deeper reductions of barriers on products of particular interest to them, such as textiles and shoes.

2) *Industrialization*

Only 7 per cent of the world's industry is now located in developing countries. The rest of the world's industry is in the rich countries. Accordingly, the developing countries are relegated to the status of "hewers of wood and drawers of water." Most of their raw materials are exported and processed in developed countries. Consequently, the employment and income which only industrialization can provide are lost.

In opposition to these trends, the Lima Declaration of March, 1975 called for a radical change so that developing countries would have 25 per cent of world industry by the year 2000. To close the gap between rich and poor the economies of the latter would have to grow faster than the economies of the former. As means to that end it was recommended that:

– A process of continuous negotiations and planning begin for the "rationalization" and redeployment of world economic activity. Rich countries are asked to "restructure" their industries in order to assist the transfer of productive capacity to developing countries.

– Rich countries vastly increase and improve the transfer of science and technology to developing countries.

– Rich countries cooperate to ensure that transnational corporations conform to the economic and social aims of developing countries in which they operate.

– Rich countries eliminate trade barriers which historically have escalated with the degree of processing of the imported item.

3) *Science and technology*

People are inclined to think of knowledge as an intangible asset derived from the inspiration of solitary genius and flowing freely throughout the world. Nothing could be further from the truth. Scientific investigations and the technology that arises from them are now the product overwhelmingly of organizations and investment. In the world in which we live this means that virtually all of this essential resource, knowledge, is developed and controlled by the rich and in particular by the huge transnational corporations which have their bases of operation in and draw their top management from the rich countries.

The new order insists that all efforts should be made to design technology corresponding to needs and conditions in developing countries, to improve their access to modern technology, and "to expand significantly the assistance from developed to developing countries in research and development programs."

A specific and, in the view of developing countries, essential part of such a program is an international code regulating the behaviour of transnational corporations. The purpose of such a code, according to the program of action, would be to:

– Prevent interference of transnationals in the internal affairs of countries where they operate.
– Regulate their activities in host countries by such measures as eliminating restrictive business practices.
– Assist in the transfer of technology and management skills to developing countries.
– Regulate the repatriation of the profits accruing from their operations and promote the re-investment of their profits in developing countries.

4) *Transfer of resources and monetary reform*
Development is about people. But to develop, people need resources – education, equipment, plant – all of which require money. Availability of capital is an essential, though not the only, requirement for development.

Financial aid has been a principal means of transferring capital to developing countries. But, as we have seen, the volume of such aid has been rising slowly and when inflation is taken into account has actually been declining. In 1974 Official Development Assistance totalled about $11 billion but in terms of

1970 prices this amounted to only $6 billion, the lowest "real" flow of the 1970s.

The debt servicing problems of developing countries continue to mount. While some of this debt has been "rescheduled," about 11 cents of every dollar earned by developing countries flows out again to pay off debts and interest. And in the case of some of the largest and poorest countries, such as India and Bangladesh, debt servicing consumes about 25 per cent of their export earnings.

The problem is even more serious than that. Far larger than interest payments has been the outflow of profits from direct investment. According to reports on seventy-three countries, this outflow was $12 billion in 1973. The combined "reverse flow" of interest and profits from developing countries amounts to about half the total flow of loans and donations received from developed countries and once again this is an overall average figure. The poorest of the developing nations have been sliding rapidly toward international financial bankruptcy.

The proposals of the New International Economic Order designed to reverse this situation include the following:

– Sizeable increase in Official Development Assistance. It is generally agreed that developing countries need and can profitably use an amount equivalent to 1 per cent of the GNP of rich countries. At the present time they receive significantly less than half this amount.

– Some mechanism for the regular if not automatic review and rescheduling of debt.

– Increasing the capitalization of such institutions as the International Development Association, the arm of the World Bank that makes loans on "softer" than commercial terms.

– Establish new channels of financial aid. Currently the most important proposal is for reform of the world reserve assets of the International Monetary Fund to permit extension of "special drawing rights" based on development requirements. In addition new mechanisms have been proposed to "re-cycle" more of the huge reserves built up by the oil-rich states to developing nations.

5) *Food production*

Agriculture lies at the heart of the development problems of many countries. It accounts for the production and income of the bulk of their populations; it is the source of food supply and raw materials for industry; and in most developing countries it is a major earner of foreign exchange and source of domestic savings. And yet, in the words of the United Nations' publication, *Background to Issues of the Seventh General Session*, "a vicious circle of poverty, underemployment, ignorance and ill-health characterize the rural sector in many developing countries, preventing the increase in production necessary to find strong and continued economic growth."

It is generally agreed that solutions to this problem lie mainly with the developing countries themselves. Specifically the increasing of production and lowering of birth rates are essential. And yet it is also clear according to the UN that "the rest of the world can provide vital support not only in the technical field but in accommodating for pressures on the country's balance of payments and in planning agricultural policy for general benefit."

In the view of developing countries any policy to be successful must stress international planning and cooperation. The period through which we are passing has been characterized by shortages, price increases, export controls, and other measures tending toward the disintegration of the world economy. The World Food Conference advanced the following specific proposals:

– An internationally managed food reserve system to guarantee supply and to moderate price fluctuations.
– A World Food Council to coordinate planning of agricultural policy.
– The channelling of far more development assistance into agriculture and rural development.

57

– Changing the production policies and consumer habits of rich countries to reflect the requirements of growing world food demands.

From confrontation to negotiation

Obviously the New International Economic Order represents an enormously complex package of proposals. Moreover, the proposals themselves are undergoing change. They are not immutable nor written in stone. And there are differences in the emphasis given to one or other parts of the proposals, among the developing countries. But whatever the mutations and qualifications these ideas represent a powerful demand for basic and far reaching reform of the international economic system.

It will therefore come as no surprise that many of the rich nations, those who have designed and benefited from the existing system, regard these reforms with considerable suspicion.

The most fundamental difference in approach between the developed and the developing concerns the degree of intervention in market forces. As we have seen, the poor countries believe generally that "market forces" is just a euphemism for the interests and privileges of the rich. These so called "market forces" kept the price of oil low for twenty-five years and this situation changed radically only when OPEC was formed and asserted itself. Also, most developed countries, including the United States and Canada, have long since developed "mixed economies" which involve some regulation of private enterprise in the public interest. The new economic order envisages no more than the same at the international level.

This difference in basic approach reveals itself time and time again in the discussion of specific proposals.

– The new economic order calls for the indexation of raw materials and manufacturers' goods; the rich countries reply that prices must be allowed to reflect market forces.
– The new economic order demands some overall agreement and international regulation of commodities; the rich countries

call for a "case by case" approach and the retention of control by national governments.

– The new economic order calls for the use of the International Monetary Fund as a development instrument; the rich countries defend its use as a central bank regulating currencies and international liquidity.

– The new economic order calls for the regulation of transnational corporations in the interest of developing countries; the rich countries defend the rights of these corporations.

These are only a few examples of the differences in approach to the basic proposal for a regulated world economy which favours, far more than does the present system, the interests of developing countries.

The opposition of the rich countries involves more than economic philosophy. Developed countries have declared that they too have specific economic problems which require recovery from the present period of recession and inflation. At the same time they note that the rules of the international game have not changed as profoundly as some developing countries believe. While the rise in oil prices has favoured OPEC, the rise in food prices – to take another essential commodity – overwhelmingly favours countries like the United States and Canada. And so, the reasoning goes, if the name of the game is confrontation poker we might see a world wide struggle of "agripower versus petropower."

Rich countries have also criticized the practicability of specific proposals of the new economic order. Such things as indexation are rejected as being next to impossible to administer or of questionable value to the poorest developing countries. Furthermore – and this is perhaps the characteristic approach of the "moderate" developed countries like Canada – it is pointed out that the implementation of reforms such as trade liberalization will take time.

A final and in many ways most deeply felt criticism of the new economic order is that it lays virtually all the blame for poverty on the rich thereby absolving the poor countries themselves of any responsibility. This feeling has been expresseed time and time again at recent international conferences. At the Population Conference in Bucharest and the Food Conference in Rome spokesmen for the rich countries called for stern measures of population control, without which, they contended, all the international reform in the world will do little good.

It is obvious from these criticisms that the proposals of the New International Economic Order will undergo a prolonged period of opposition and struggle and modification. But there is some evidence that progress is being made. When this comprehensive program of reform was first introduced at the Sixth Special Session in May 1974, the mood was one of declaration and confrontation. Although the New International Economic Order was actually born at this Session, it was regarded as just another document. In a sense the developing countries were concerned with only one thing – placing their message before the world in the most unequivocal terms.

Producing a new mood . . .

In the interval between the Sixth and Seventh Special Sessions an extraordinary number of publications, studies, and conferences produced a new mood among Western leaders. The dominant message of urgency in international development was summed up in *Mankind at the Turning Point*, by Mihajlo Mesarovic and Eduard Pestel, a sequel to the Club of Rome's seminal book, *Limits to Growth*. Mesarovic and Pestel said the longer the rich nations postpone the massive effort in speeding up development through better trade and monetary structures, the more costly the penalty will be for both developing and developed. "There is no more urgent task in the quest for peace than to help guide the world system onto the path of organic growth through the various stages of its evolution through cooperation rather than confrontation."

The Dag Hammarskjöld Foundation, drawing on experts around the world, held several seminars and issued a report *What Now*. The choice is cooperation or world chaos, the Foundation said, urging "a political commitment to set in motion the process of change."

This work was paralleled by a multinational team organized by the Aspen Institute for Humanistic Studies in the United States, which put forward a plan for a "planetary bargain" among rich and poor nations. The bargain would begin with a commitment by nations to provide people everywhere with basic human needs and would be carried on in part by "extra national commissions" empowered by the governments creating them to function at a "political" level. Essentially, the planetary bargain would be a trade-off between self-reliance of the developing and self-restraint of the developed.

The Institute on Man and Science, meeting at Rensselaerville, New York, threw its weight behind plans to restructure the United Nations in order to achieve more global economic cooperation. The principal aim of a new world economic bargain, director Richard N. Gardner said in a report, *New Structures for Economic Interdependence*, should not be the transfer of wealth from developed to developing countries. Rather it should be the internalizing of the wealth creating process within the developing countries, the fairer distribution of wealth within both rich and poor countries, and the elimination of poverty everywhere."

Meanwhile, nine European Economic Community (EEC) (Common Market) nations quietly negotiated a five-year treaty with forty-six developing nations in Africa, the Caribbean and the Pacific (ACP) that offered a model for the future. The agreement included provisions on terms of trade, an export revenue stabilization plan, financial plans, and industrial cooperation.

The Lomé Treaty (so-called because it was signed in the capital of Togo) includes these features:

– All ACP industrial goods and 96 per cent of agricultural products will enter the EEC tariff-free. This will encourage the poor nations to develop industries.
– A fund of $450 million is established to compensate the ex-

porters of twelve primary products (peanuts, cocoa, coffee, cotton, coconuts, palm nuts and kernels, hides and skins, timber products, bananas, tea, raw sisal, and iron ore) if prices fall below an average price. This ground-breaking program, "Stabex," gives the developing nations some defense against a wayward market place that can double raw material prices one year and halve them the next.

What Lomé showed was that practical agreements with the Third and Fourth Worlds are possible without confrontation. Encouraged, the Common Market Commission began exploring how Lomé ideas could be used world-wide.

Of equal significance was a report *Towards a New International Economic Order* by a group of ten experts commissioned by the Commonwealth Heads of Government. The Commonwealth team backed the integrated commodities program of the United Nations Conference on Trade and Development (UNCTAD), indexation, producer associations, trade liberalization through GATT, and a target of Official Development Assistance of 1 per cent of GNP by 1980. The special value of this report was the consensus expressed by the developed and developing within the Commonwealth. The Canadian government swallowed hard in giving "whole-hearted support ... for the approach and thrust" of the report, which it commended to the UN. Canada's own strategy, published shortly after the Commonwealth report came out, lagged several steps behind (see Chapter 6).

Lomé and the Commonwealth gains were important. But the vital component in any move to a new economic order is unquestionably the United States, the most powerful economic force in the world. And at the Sixth Special Session, the United States did not like the Group of Seventy-Seven ganging up on the West and passing resolutions whose strength lay not in the realities of power but in mere numerical superiority at the UN. This led to the famous "tyranny of the majority" charge the US hurled at the Third World, an unfortunate bit of invective because it hardened American attitudes (still in a bad state over

Vietnam, Watergate, and the recession) against the United Nations. The New International Economic Order, United States Ambassador John Scali told the closing Sixth Session, "does not represent unanimity of opinion in this Assembly. To label some of these highly controversial conclusions as agreed is not only idle, it is self-deceiving." Canada and other Western nations also entered strong reservations.

As the Seventh Special Session opened, everyone at the UN was on edge, waiting to see if the US would let the other shoe drop, thus effectively killing the new economic order. But Secretary of State Kissinger, apparently persuaded that the developing world's clamour was undermining Washington's claim to any moral world leadership, surprised everyone. Kissinger was detained in the Middle East but assigned the new US Ambassador, Daniel Moynihan, to read his address (one hour and forty-five minutes long) which promised a better deal than ever for the developing world. A series of development proposals was launched centring around the creation within the International Monetary Fund of a $10 billion lending agency to stabilize the export earnings of developing countries. "We have heard your voices," the United States declared, "We embrace your hopes. We will join your efforts."

The consensus document which emerged from the two weeks of hard bargaining was in reality less than a genuine consensus but still more than a unilateral declaration by developing countries. Perhaps the most significant thing was that all parties had settled down to the negotiation of the same major items. But the language of the final document reveals that the process of creating a new economic order has only begun.

On trade liberalization developed countries declared their intention to remove barriers "where feasible and appropriate," those countries which had not previously accepted targets for the increase of official development assistance undertook to "make their best efforts," the Special Drawing Rights (SDR) aid link would "form part of the considerations" of the International Monetary Fund, the various options for preserving the purchasing power of developing countries "need to be further studied." On the subject of multinational corporations, developed countries pledged to "encourage whenever possible" their enterprises to conform to the objectives of developing countries.

Given the ambiguity of this language and the fact that even so a number of developed countries felt obliged to enter reservations about the final document, it is hardly surprising that the consensus was supported by the Group of Seventy-Seven by only the barest of margins. And yet by contrast with the confrontation at the Sixth Special Session this undertaking seemed a step toward common interest and cooperation between rich and poor. In the words of Jan Pronk, the Netherlands' Minister of Development, this was "the message for the future."

PART THREE: WHAT CANADA IS DOING

Chapter 5

The Haunting Question of Aid

For generations the fishermen of Senegal, a small country of four million people on the coast of West Africa, set out each morning in fleets of *pirogues*, a sort of dugout canoe. The paddling was hard and strong backs were needed but, after all, that was the way their fathers and their fathers' fathers fished. But gradually it became apparent that not enough fish were being caught to feed the increasing population.

In 1969, the government of Senegal began a four-year development plan, emphasizing rural development. One of the objectives was to speed up the modernization of traditional fishing methods without destroying those traditions. The answer lay not in huge fishing vessels but in outboard motors for the *pirogues*. Canada was asked to provide 3,500 motors and to help build and equip maintenance workshops. The government of Canada agreed and provided $2.7 million in interest-free loans and $400,000 in grant funds. Another CIDA project was under way.

The Canadian International Development Agency, organized in 1968 as a successor to the old External Aid office, administers about $1 billion annually in government assistance to developing countries (about one-fifth what Canadians spend on liquor). Canada ranks seventh as a donor among the eighteen rich countries forming the Development Assistance Committee (DAC) of the Organization for Economic Cooperation and Development. Total DAC assistance is $26 billion annually, which seems like a big sum until it is compared with the $245 billion spent annually throughout the world on military armaments.

At any one time CIDA manages or monitors some 2,000 projects of a very diversified nature in seventy-six countries located from three to five thousand miles from CIDA headquarters in Ottawa where 1,000 persons are employed. It contributes to multilateral agencies, such as United Nations development programs, and supports non-governmental organizations in Canada and abroad which mobilize a multimillion dollar effort by the private sector.

Canadian aid is increasing rapidly. In 1974, total Canadian disbursements – public and private – to developing countries reached $1.6 billion, a 52 per cent jump over the previous year. Viewed against our national capacity, Canadian government assistance was 0.52 per cent of the gross national product. (The UN has urged developed countries to donate 0.7 per cent of GNP). Three cents out of each Canadian tax dollar goes to development assistance.

This money is used for power development; increasing water supply; communications and transportation equipment; agriculture, education, and health projects; industry, mining, and construction; food aid; emergency relief; commodity loans and lines of credit; and research projects.

Development, of course, is not only dollars. Over the past decade, tens of thousands of Canadians have served overseas as teachers, experts, or advisers under contract to CIDA, as employees of Canadian companies hired to carry out CIDA-financed projects, or as volunteers for non-governmental organizations active in developing countries.

Bilateral aid
The largest part of our assistance (60 per cent) is extended bilaterally from Canada directly to the recipient country. The

choice of recipients reflects a mixture of political, economic, and developmental considerations, including the important desire to concentrate our resources in order to make them more effective. Increasingly, aid projects will be concentrated in the Fourth World.

The criteria for assistance have until now, been somewhat vague but included the specific needs of the country, its balance of payments position, ability to utilize Canadian resources effectively, the political importance attached to economic development, and the historical ties Canada has with the country.

Two-thirds of our assistance goes to only ten countries – India, Bangladesh, Pakistan, Indonesia, Nigeria, Tunisia, Ghana, Tanzania, Niger, and Sri Lanka. As this list indicates, our greatest commitment has been to the South Asian subcontinent of India, Bangladesh, Pakistan, and Sri Lanka. This reflects the Commonwealth connection, the huge population and great poverty of the area as well as the recent succession of disasters in that part of the world. Non-food aid to India has been cut back, however, to protest India's development and explosion of an atomic bomb using Canadian material.

Two of the fastest growing areas of Canadian aid programs have been those of Africa, especially Francophone Africa, and Latin America. Much of Africa falls into the Fourth World category where assistance may mean the difference between life and death. For example, a number of recipient countries are located in the Sahelian belt which has been devastated by drought over the past several years.

The expansion of our Latin American programs has been somewhat more controversial. It began following a 1973 visit to the region by the president of CIDA, and according to one report, pressure from the Department of Industry, Trade and Commerce which is interested in commercial relations with "middle-income" developing countries such as Mexico, Argentina, and Brazil. The interest of Quebec in Latin America and the desire to expand our Francophone programs seem also to have been factors.

Finally, we should mention the Caribbean program which, while small in dollar amounts, is the largest per capita recipient of Canadian aid. Our interest in that region reflects various historic ties not least being sizeable Canadian private investment. The thrust of our program – not entirely successful – has been to assist the islands towards some larger economic or political federation.

Multilateral aid

While direct Canada-to-Country aid is still our most important channel of assistance, we have been steadily increasing our contributions to such international organizations as the World Bank and the various UN agencies. This has been in response to the expressed desires of developing countries as well as the recognition that large-scale development programs can only be mounted successfully through cooperation among countries.

By far the largest recipient of Canadian multilateral assistance is the International Development Association, the arm of the World Bank, which lends funds on the softest terms – low interest rates, fifty years to pay, ten years grace – to developing countries. These funds are overwhelmingly invested in the "least developed countries" which have greatest difficulty in securing commercial investment. Of late, the Canadian government has strongly supported the establishment and growth of regional development funds such as the Asian, Caribbean and the Inter American Development Banks. These have the advantage of size combined with being close to the peculiar development problems of different parts of the world.

And finally, of course, Canada has been and remains a major contributor to the United Nations' group of institutions, most importantly the United Nations Development Program, the World Food Program, and UNESCO. For example, Canada made a grant of $3 million to the World Health Organization for the control of river blindness in West Africa, an affliction estimated to cause the total or partial blindness of 70,000 people per year.

Canada has generally attempted to provide assistance in areas where we believe that we have a special competence, for example, transport and communications, fertilizer and raw materials, and food aid. We have also strongly supported energy development by providing generating units for India's Kundah dam, transmission lines in Tunisia and so on. Besides these investments in the "physical plant" of development we have stressed human development in our health and educational assistance programs. At the present time the largest single group of Canadian advisers abroad are teachers in Francophone Africa.

The forms of assistance
Whatever the area of the world or development problem, our assistance is extended in three main forms – food aid, people, and money. Each of these illustrates the complexity and contradictions of development assistance.

1. *Food aid*
Our largest single commodity program is food. Between 1970 and 1974 we provided approximately $340 million in food aid through the World Food Program and our bilateral programs. While this assistance had its origins partly in our selfish desire to dispose of surplus farm products, it has continued into this period of sellers' market.

In response to the critical food shortages in the Sahel region and the Indian sub-continent, and the balance of payments difficulties experienced by many of Canada's food recipients with the increase in oil prices, disbursements on bilateral food aid almost doubled from 1973 to 1974.

In addition a major new commitment was announced by External Affairs Minister Allan MacEachen at the 1974 World Food Conference in Rome, covering the years 1975 – 78. This entails one million tons of grain per year for three years; an increase to $45 million annually in non-grain foodstuffs such as fish, milk powder, beans, and rapeseed; and an increase to at least 20 per cent of our food aid disbursed through multilateral channels.

"We are doing what we can to fend off the threat of starvation in those areas most severely affected," MacEachen noted, "but, if anything, such rearguard action has made us painfully aware of the urgent need for massive investment in agricultural production and rural development in most developing countries."

He said that CIDA would step up such specific development aid as the provision of fertilizer, research in dryland farming, water resource harnessing, wheat farming, cattle and dairy farming, crop storage facilities, fisheries and forestry management, soil sciences, and animal nutrition and breeding.

2. *People*

The second form of Canadian assistance is people – engineers, teachers, doctors, bureaucrats, scientists – generally speaking, highly-trained people who are in short supply in the least developed countries. In fact the number of such Canadians abroad under contract with CIDA began to decrease after 1972. In that year there were 1,130, in 1973, 974 and in 1974, 874 – 40 per cent of whom were teaching in French-speaking African countries. The reasons for the decline are several, including the greater number of locally trained people, the high cost of such people and the sensitivity of developing countries to their presence.

Because CIDA contract personnel are paid at Canadian rates, a developing country gets one Canadian for the price of two people from Britain or three from another part of the Third World. As for the local sensitivities, this reflects in part an understandable if sometimes excessive xenophobia on the part of developing countries as well as too frequent examples of "cultural imperialism" on the part of our people. One survey of opinion reported that our "mature experts" were judged insensitive to the local culture, unwilling to listen, and generally inclined to retreat into an affluent expatriate "colony" of their own.

Such an assessment of Canadians overseas is manifestly unfair to those who do live among the people they have gone abroad to help; and it certainly should not be applied to most of the workers recruited by the Canadian University Service Overseas (CUSO), whom we will meet in the next chapter. But there is a general impression that the standard of living of CIDA contract personnel is too high to fit the life of developing countries. Briefing for Canadians going abroad is slowly being improved, however. A group of miners and their families going to India to assist in the second phase of a training project at the Khetri copper mine were briefed before leaving Sudbury on what to expect in their posting. In the Latin America program, CIDA workers and their families now receive Spanish-language training in Guatemala for an eight to ten week period.

3. *Money*

Developing countries have a strong preference for the third form of aid – money – which they can deploy with greatest flexibility. Judged by international standards, Canadian financial assistance has been excellent. In 1973, for example, nearly half our program consisted of outright grants while most of the loans were on the softest terms – no interest, ten years grace, fifty years to repay. These funds are of the utmost importance to the poorest countries which, having suffered chronic and recently acute balance of payments deficits, labour under huge and mounting external debts.

Canada's general policy is to relate the terms of assistance to the need of the country concerned. Most of CIDA's program consists of grants and advances, given both bilaterally and multilaterally. In 1974, forty-five development loans totalling $184 million were made, only seven of which were on the hard terms of thirty years maturity, seven years grace and thirty years to repay, and thirty-eight loans on the soft terms. Maximum soft terms (called concessionality) are especially important because of the alarming rate at which the indebtedness of developing countries has been growing. Compared with the terms offered by the US, the United Kingdom, France, Germany, and Japan, Canada's efforts are regarded as very generous.

Assistance to foreign students, emergency aid, export credits, and international research development are other ways the Canadian government helps the Third World.

The main channel of Canadian assistance to research is the International Development Research Centre (IDRC), which was set up as a public corporation by parliament in 1970. The Centre, with headquarters in Ottawa, is the managing agent for certain projects that are jointly funded by other organizations, such as the Ford Foundation. Its own funds all come from parliament and the current budget of $27 million is part of the CIDA total. The Board of Governors (eleven of whom are Canadian and ten non-Canadian) is responsible for 302 projects in seventy-five countries costing $47 million. Most of these projects are in the fields of agriculture, rural health care, and low-cost housing.

"Perhaps most important of all," notes Clyde Sanger, IDRC's information officer, "it has great flexibility because its funds are completely untied. It can pay for a Swedish architect to adapt a 'compost toilet,' widely used in rural parts of Sweden, to the tropical climate of Tanzania; or for an Australian plant breeder who has experimented for years with pasture legumes in dry parts of Queensland to use his knowledge for the benefit of Caribbean islanders who want to improve the pastures on their coral soils."

Adding up our aid
What does all this aid add up to? Is enough Canadian money being spent on development? Are the CIDA projects successful? Are poverty-stricken people and countries actually being helped to develop themselves through this Canadian effort? And what about the charge I have heard at international conferences that the developed countries have received more economic benefits from aid programs than the beneficiaries themselves?

Those are the questions I ask myself continually as I sit on the External Affairs Subcommittee on International Development. It is almost impossible to give general answers about CIDA. The journalist Richard Gwyn noted, "hardly anyone knows how its vast budget is spent, on what, or why, whether well or badly." This situation has led to a number of highly critical articles about CIDA and its operation. In turn this focused attention in parliament on CIDA's mistakes, drawing attention away from the very real need of evaluating CIDA with respect to Canada's overall goal of helping the developing world. Ironically, CIDA personnel themselves have for a long time been warning against reliance on aid programs as a measure of our assistance. "The message is all too clear," CIDA president Paul Gerin-Lajoie has insisted, "there is not enough aid and aid is not enough." CIDA's strategy plans for 1975 – 80 are to provide aid within the context of an integrated government plan, involving support of the trade and monetary reforms of the New International Economic Order (see Chapter 6).

Before asking questions about the value of CIDA, we should remind ourselves that development is not a gimmick, a neat gadget invented once and for all. It is a process of discovery in a labyrinth of complexities.

Mistakes have been made and continue to be made. Some of the mistakes have come from our own stupidity and selfishness, some from the stupidity and selfishness of recipients. But many mistakes were made honestly, on the basis of then prevailing ideas or beliefs which have since proved inadequate. CIDA leadership can be criticized, but it should not be condemned. The question now is whether they – and all of us – show the willingness and ability to move forward.

CIDA admits its evaluation procedures are weak. Though some projects are successes and others failures the overall impact cannot be measured with a slide rule. Development assistance may be a minor factor in the economies of developing countries but surely the Third and Fourth Worlds would be even poorer today without this international effort over the past twenty-five years. Development assistance has intangible dimensions, often facilitating local experiments and reforms.

Gérin-Lajoie believes that development assistance "has been one of the most concrete expressions of the moral cognizance that we are one world in development, interdependent and ideally concerned with the lot of the less fortunate. Through development assistance, more people than ever before have come to understand more clearly the lot of their fellow man."

This expression of noble purpose must be blended with some hard political judgements. Until this year, it was required that about two-thirds of the total bilateral funds had to be spent in Canada. This is called "tied aid." For example, the outboard motors helping the Senegal fishermen increase their yield were all purchased in Canada. Thus, in a very real way, foreign aid is good for the Canadian economy.

Gérin-Lajoie himself emphasized this in a speech in 1973 to the Montreal Board of Trade when he said that in a three-year period CIDA funds had served to buy $251 million worth of Canadian foodstuffs and $155 million worth of Canadian commodities, as well as millions more in Short Take Off and Landing (STOL) aircraft and communications equipment. It was in businessmen's interests to support CIDA, he said, because "if CIDA were to close down or reduce its programs of development assistance abroad, the Canadian economy would suffer considerable strain both in terms of markets and in terms of jobs."

This, of course, leads into questions of CIDA contracts and how they are obtained, along with questions of why one country is helped and another is not. The Parliamentary Subcommittee is rightly concerned with all these matters. What it all indicates is that aid is an extremely complicated business, whose nobility of purpose has been politically sweetened by the boost it gives the Canadian economy. It would not be difficult to make the case that the $3.6 billion Canada has spent on international development in the past twenty-five years has helped the domestic economy by at least an equivalent amount when added employment, personal and corporate income tax, disposal of surpluses, and development of new trading partners are considered.

On the other hand tied aid is not necessarily a bad thing. It would be pushing altruism a bit far to provide loans or grants to a country for equipment – and then have that country make the purchase in a market Canada is competing against. Canada, in fact, tries to extend technological and material assistance as part of its bilateral financing. An example of this is the assistance Canada is supplying to the Zambia Railways. A team of management and technical experts are managing the railway and training personnel to take over these functions. At the same time rolling stock, including tank cars, cement cars, and refrigerated containers are being sent from Canada to increase the railway's capacity to move freight.

Nonetheless, the fact that so much Canadian aid is tied reveals that Canada is not as generous as appears on the surface. Developing countries complain that tied aid reduces their buying power in world markets and locks them into sometimes inefficient development projects.

In short, Canadian aid has long been designed to be of substantial direct help to our own country as well as the Third World. This led the Subcommittee on International Development, which issued a report in 1971, to urge the government "to proceed without delay to untie Canadian funds for procurement in other developing countries." The first move in this direction is now contained in the new Five-Year Strategy (1975 – 80), allowing the untying of bilateral development loans so that suppliers in developing countries will be eligible to compete for contracts. This is not as significant as it appears at first glance because in most cases industries in developing countries are not able to compete economically with Canadian suppliers. The government itself notes: "On the basis of experience in the U.S.A., which untied to developing countries several years ago, the government is convinced that adhering to this Understanding would have minimal effects on Canadian exporters."

In addition to this modest gesture the government will consider untying to suppliers in rich countries "in selected cases." Such cases would be where there was an urgent need for assistance which Canada could not supply and where the benefits to development outweigh the impact "on specific sectors" of the Canadian economy. That is the crunch. It seems clear that the government is attempting to move gradually to further untying but how far it gets will depend on the resistance of Canadian business.

The haunting question
Much more than improved bilateral aid is needed. Nothing shows this more clearly than food aid. The World Food Conference came at a time when famine in Africa and Asia was widespread: television conveyed grim pictures of starving children; and Members of Parliament received thousands of letters from Canadians who wanted the government to help.

People somehow have the idea that help can be instant. Call it red tape or international procedures, the fact is that aid programs take months and even years to organize and carry out. The commitment that Canada made would take at least a year to begin to be implemented. Moreover, 60 per cent of the pledged food would be sent abroad under bilateral agreements and of this amount some 80 per cent of the food would end up being sold – not given – to local people. This is by no means illegal. For years, Canada has been donating food to developing countries and allowing the country to sell the food in order to protect local markets and to build up counterpart funds for development projects.

The answer to the food problem is to help the countries produce their own, but this means they must have adequate supplies of fertilizer, which requires energy, which in turn requires sufficient capital or credits. Canadians should be told that if they really want to help that starving child they see on TV, they should support the UN's call for a new economic order, since it is the present economic disorder that is penalizing the child by withholding from him what he has a right to.

In addition to regulations that may or may not be of benefit to people, food aid is subject to smuggling, black markets, and profiteering. Among other effects, this undermines public confidence among Canadians that aid is getting through to those for whom it is intended.

This was one of the reasons that prompted Gerin-Lajoie personally to investigate conditions in Bangladesh a few months before the bloody coup of 1975. About $40 million of Canadian food has been sent annually to Bangladesh, which is perhaps the most desperate country in the entire world. An estimated seventy-three million people are crowded into 55,000 square miles making Bangladesh, at 1,400 people per square mile, one of the world's most densely populated countries with one of the highest population growth rates. The combination of large population, very limited natural resources, and the country's susceptibility to cyclones, floods, and drought has worked in vicious proportions to impoverish the Bangladesh people, whose annual per capita income is only $70.

Gerin-Lajoie returned from Bangladesh apparently convinced that local police were stepping up measures against smugglers and profiteers. He assigned CIDA personnel to supervise the unloading of Canadian shipments. But his report opened up questions far larger than smuggling.

"What is the sense of massive food aid that seems to succeed only in prolonging the sentence of individuals already definitely condemned by malnutrition?" he asked. The food rationing system is biased toward the haves, not the have-nots. "Despite some recent improvements, the rural landless – most of them without work – get an extremely meagre share of the rationed food, while the system takes care first of the urban areas and, within rural areas, gives priority to the army, teachers and public servants." He recommended that Canada urge the directing of rationed food to the poorest segments of society.

Gerin-Lajoie's trip to Bangladesh raised the most haunting of all the aid questions: does aid to the Third World – without stamping out the causes of the poverty in the first place – only prolong pain and suffering? He told of visiting an orphanage for children whose parents were victims of recent floods:

"It was one of the most rending experiences of my life. If they survive childhood, these children, who are given two meagre meals per day, will possibly never gain the health and strength to live normal human lives...In the face of this situation, the answer that I found could not be in terms of simple pity, cold logic or a philosophical view of death. I found the answer in the looks of these orphans – their silent yet seemingly indomitable will to live."

The spirit of survival in the Third World was eloquently summed up by a Bengali doctor, the manager of a modest rural medical centre, who told the CIDA president: "We know our problems; we have also learned the solutions. If you wish to help us gather our strength and rebuild our pride, stop crying over our dead. But rather, in a brotherly spirit, provide us with the resources which we might use to ensure our development in our own way."

It is all very well to say that all aid perpetuates dependency and must give way to structural reforms for full international development. The fact is that for at least the next decade we will need to emphasize both trade and aid if the poorest billion people in the thirty-five least developed countries are not to fall even further behind. In fact the World Bank predicts that between $30 and $40 billion, mostly in highly concessional form, will be needed in the years 1976 – 80 *in addition* to current flows. "What is needed by 1980," says CIDA's president, "is a mobilization of efforts far beyond anything we have seen up to now."

Is CIDA a success? Ask the fishermen of Senegal now fishing in their motorized *pirogues*. It took a long time to get the program set up, but shortly after the full fleet of 4,800 *pirogues* became operational, yields doubled and revenues tripled. The number of fishermen grew from 30,000 to 33,000.

The success of this CIDA project has not only had a significant impact on Senegal's economy but has also improved the status of the fishermen. Passing from barter to a cash economy and from individual work to cooperative methods, they have been able to take development in their own hands.

Chapter 6

Speeding Up the Five-Year Strategy

Jacob Javits, the burly senior Senator from New York, was speaking. Around the table in the conference room of the Canadian Mission at the United Nations sat a dozen US Senators and Congressmen and Canadian M.P.s. The Seventh Special Session of the UN was in full swing, grappling with the Group of Seventy-Seven's working paper on the New International Economic Order, and the American and Canadians had decided to examine our role as politicians.

"You're a bridge to every important group in the world," Senator Javits said, looking directly at the Canadian parliamentarians. "You're a bridge between the United States and the developing world. You're a bridge to the European Common Market. In fact, you're the best bridge there is between the developed and developing nations."

Senator Charles Percy from Illinois backed him up. "Canada is the honest broker of the world," he insisted.

The Canadian M.P.s looked a little uncomfortable. Was this more American hyperbole? Are we really that important? Or did the US legislators really mean that Canada was in the best position to sell the American viewpoint on development?

Not only the M.P.s but the whole government has reason to

feel distinctly uncomfortable about Canada's changing role in international development.

Only a couple of days before our meeting, External Affairs Minister Allan MacEachen had unveiled a Five-Year (1975–80) Canadian Strategy for International Development Cooperation. That strategy took the big step forward that many aid experts had been calling for: a commitment to structural reform along with increased aid, meaning that Canada was ready to move forward on commodity agreements, trade liberalization and industrial cooperation.

But the Canadian Strategy was much weaker in specifics than a report on the implementation of a new economic order commissioned by the Commonwealth heads of government. Canada was part of the Commonwealth team that prepared the report – and here we were several paces behind the Commonwealth.

MacEachen and the M.P.s knew there was practically no public opinion in Canada supporting the new Strategy, largely because the Canadian public is so poorly informed on what the new economic order is all about. If Canada did accept the Commonwealth conclusions and pressed ahead in an international leadership role, and a backlash developed at home when the people start to realize the personal cost involved, the Canadian "bridge" might turn out to be pretty shaky.

Also, two-thirds of Canada's trade is with the United States. Can we realistically expect to alter trading patterns to help the developing world without the full support of the US itself? It goes without saying that Canada does not want to be an international mouthpiece for the United States. We have our own viewpoint that recognizes the validity of the Seventy-Seven's demand for structural changes in international economic relations – but how forceful can we be in implementing change when we are so dependent on the US?

And, the final discomfort, Canada (as well as the US) is so preoccupied with inflation, unemployment, and housing shortages at home that any major effort to help the developing nations at this moment seems destined to failure. Better, therefore, to go along with the prevailing UN mood for change but keep a low profile. Slow progress. Make sure the piers are strong before we start to assemble the bridge. Is that the Canadian way? Moderation? Caution? Or just plain realism, recognizing that illusions of grandeur could be quickly shattered by the big boys of the economic world?

Zeroing in on a practical analysis of Canada's leadership potential, MacEachen has pointed out that External Affairs can huff and puff all it wants to; but without the support of the big financial guns in the Canadian government – the Departments of Finance and Industry, Trade and Commerce – rhetoric is the only accomplishment. And these departments will only give their support when they see the detailed changes called for in the new order in the light of Canada's self-interest. However, just as "foreign aid" has always been sold to the public as being good for Canada, so too can the new economic order.

Nonetheless, a new direction for Canada in international development has been charted by Prime Minister Pierre Trudeau. His celebrated speech at the Mansion House, London, in the spring of 1975, was an eloquent appeal for a new ethic of sharing by the developed. "The demands of the developing countries have been carefully formulated and powerfully articulated," he said. "They reflect a sense of frustration and anger. Those countries seek no piecemeal adjustments but a comprehensive restructuring of all the components – fiscal, monetary, trade, transport and investment. The response of the industrialized countries can be no less well-prepared and no less comprehensive in scope."

Canada unquestionably has a leadership role to play in international development and it would be tragic in the light of alarming world conditions for us to go soft on our responsibilities. We have a new national policy – and it is up to politicians, the media, the Churches, businessmen, labour, agriculture, educators, and all those interested in the viability of modern society to understand it and see how it can be implemented and strengthened.

The Five-Year Strategy

The Five-Year Strategy begins by acknowledging that Canada, as one of the most prosperous nations in the world, has both the responsibility and ability to make a meaningful contribution to the improvement of conditions in the developing world.

"As a country with an impressive resource base, Canada has generally benefited from the sharp rise in the prices of primary commodities. Shortfalls in world food production, in particular, have increased our grain exports and the prices paid for these on the world market. It is thus inevitable, no matter how badly we may view the domestic situation, that in the eyes of a hungry developing world Canada will be singled out in the future by the rest of the world to assume a great responsibility to share its food and agricultural commodities with the developing countries, as only one of four net food exporting nations."

Besides – and here the Strategy reverts to the self-interest argument – the development assistance program "can have catalytic and positive effects on the Canadian economy." The goods and services procured in Canada strengthen industry here, create jobs for Canadians, maintain support for the aid program, and develop interests in overseas markets. All this, the Strategy admits, indicates that the cost of the aid program to Canadian society is less than volume alone could suggest. (Speaking of discomfiture in the Canadian position, this argument makes me very uncomfortable, but I am enough of a politician to recognize its necessity.)

Then the Strategy makes the point that although Canada's commercial links with the Third World are weak, Canada is potentially important to the Third World. "Its past development assistance program, as well as its lack of imperial or colonial ambitions, has gained Canada a favourable reputation on a relatively progressive and unbiased participant in Third World Affairs." Canada has been in the forefront of responding to the emergency facing the developing countries as a result of the oil, fertilizer, and food crises. Accordingly, the Strategy highlights these steps:

– Canada will develop new forms of cooperation with developing countries that are benefiting from increased revenues from oil or other commodities, which will take into account their improved balance of payments position.

– Development assistance programs must be focused increasingly on lower-income developing countries with highest priority to projects that will improve the living and working conditions of the least privileged sections of their population.

– The government reaffirms its determination to achieve the official United Nations target of 0.7 per cent of GNP and to move towards this target by annual increases.

– The Canadian program will focus on fewer sectors for greater quality and efficient use of expertise. Such crucial sectors will include food production and distribution, rural development, education and training, public health and demography, and shelter and energy.

– Ninety per cent of the bilateral program will be concessional. Most loans will be provided at zero per cent interest, ten years grace and fifty years maturity. Loans at 3 per cent interest, with seven years grace and thirty years maturity, will be made to countries in the upper range of the development spectrum.

– The government will partially untie its bilateral development loans by permitting third world procurement (as we saw in Chapter 5).

– The government will maintain its program of food aid, including the provision of one million tons of grain per year for the three year period 1975 – 78. Up to 20 per cent of the food aid program will be available for procurement in third countries, mainly in the developing world, when difficulties of transport and supply are present.

Beyond these reforms in aid, the Strategy recognizes the need for a new multidimensional approach to development.

In part, this springs from a growing recognition of Canada's important similarities with the developing countries. For example, we, too, are a significant exporter of primary commodities and need stable marketing arrangements; we are concerned with upgrading our natural resources prior to export as well as protecting our sovereignty over natural resources. Thus, in both diversifying and extending our economic relationships, we ought to be strengthening our links with developing countries.

But our changing policy is based not only on our self-interest but also on the growing militancy of developing nations. The Strategy document says, "These countries have made clear that while they will continue to seek a greater volume and higher quality of development assistance, their fundamental concern is to modify substantially the pattern of their economic relations with the industrialized world."

In responding to this concern, Canada has set a new course: "The government undertakes to harmonize various external and domestic policies which have an impact on the developing countries, and to use a variety of policy instruments in the trade, international monetary, and other fields in order to achieve its international development objectives."

The basic question is how far we are prepared to go towards meeting these objectives.

Trade liberalization

As we have seen trade is a major, one might even say, *the* major item on the agenda of the New International Economic Order. Its long term potential for financing development is far greater than official development assistance and it has the added appeal to both developing and developed countries of being a "pay your own way" approach to development.

At the present time Canadian trade with developing countries is a significant though not a major item. In 1974 developing countries supplied 7 per cent of our imports and took 10 per cent of our exports. Their exports to us represented only 2 per cent of their total export trade. Clearly, developing countries are not about to replace the US as our major trading partner and yet, in the words of the Economic Council of Canada, "growing two-way trade between rich countries and the developing countries should be welcomed as an opportunity as well as a competitive challenge to Canadians."

While the Canadian government has made some modest efforts in this direction, our policy is still constricted by various obstacles. For example, as part of the GATT policy of opening markets gradually to developing countries, Canada passed into law in July 1974 the *Generalized System of Preferences for Developing Countries* (GSP). This extends tariff preferences – that is, lower than average but not zero tariffs – to a wide range of manufactured and semi-manufactured goods from developing countries. In its first year of operation this had a modest positive effect on our trade with developing countries, but several "loopholes" in the law diminish its potential.

In the first place, it does not apply to agricultural and food products, though Canada has extended and is further extending some preferences to unprocessed "tropical products." In the second place, the GSP exempts a certain select list of textile products, footwear, and electronic equipment. These items, of great interest to developing countries because they most clearly reflect their comparative advantage in labour-intensive industry, are subject to bilateral import quotas. And finally the entire scheme is subject to "safeguard provisions" under which the preferential rates can be withdrawn when imports reach certain levels or threaten injury to domestic producers.

Granted that loss of revenue or jobs is not an appealing prospect, what can be done to transform this situation? The answer or at least the theory behind the answer is beginning to emerge. Mr. MacEachen has advanced a scenario in which Canada would move gradually out of the lower-technology, labour-intensive activities and into a role as part of the "arsenal" for world development. "Quebec workers might then be manufacturing rice-cultivation machines for Bangladesh instead of textiles; Maritime industries might be supplying mass-produced pumps for the Sahel irrigation network and fish processing plants for the West African coast; Prairie manufacturers might have become suppliers of agricultural inputs – from tractors to fertilizers – for much of the Indian subcontinent."

The logic underlying this proposal – of Canada transforming its traditional activities of fishing or farming into new knowledge-intensive industries supplying world development – is clear and compelling. But how do you convert all of the "mights" in Mr. MacEachen's speech into realities? In my view that is the real crunch. Economic vision of this sort requires long-term planning, hard decisions, boldness and commitment. Transforming our economy will require powerful and coordinated adjustment assistance programs. To date our programs have been neither. We must decide whether we really intend gradually to phase out our weak industries or to keep them struggling along.

Commodities

A basic objective of the New International Economic Order is to improve the stability and terms of trade of the raw material exports of developing countries. The Canadian policy on the subject of commodities can only be described as ambivalent and cautious. While we have supported "just and equitable prices" for raw materials we have not supported the principle that a basic objective of commodity agreements must be sustained improvement in the terms of trade of developing countries. While the Prime Minister in his 1975 Mansion House speech said that "we must aim for nothing less than an acceptable distribution of the world's wealth," in the 1973 sugar negotiations Canada opposed a price agreement that would have guaranteed the 1975 real purchasing power of sugar at the 1953 level!

Canada's response to the proposals of an integrated commodity approach has been lukewarm at best. We have consistently refused to support producers associations, preferring instead the US approach of producer-consumer forums. Accordingly, we have refused to join recently-formed iron and copper producer associations.

The same caution characterizes our response to other key features of an integrated program. We have said that we are "prepared to examine" commodity agreements for a wide range of products, that buffer stocks "may be an appropriate technique" and that the concept of a common fund to finance these stocks is "certainly worth examination." But when it comes to the key requirement of improving the terms of trade of developing countries our caution becomes something approaching opposition. We insist that commodity prices must reflect market forces, but we do not concede that those forces largely reflect the interests and power of the rich. And while we do not wish to see low commodity prices, we have "considerable doubts" about indexation.

It would be a relief if we could claim that Canada's ambivalence toward the New International Economic Order is only the reflection of reactionary and obsolete ideas at work in our society. Unfortunately, the ambivalence is built into our economic and political position in the world. While we are a major exporter of some raw materials and thus share the interests of some developing countries we are also a major importer of other commodities – for example bauxite, coffee, and sugar – and so wish to protect our consumers. Furthermore most of our raw material exports – food, petroleum, copper and iron ore – go to our major trading partners, the US, Europe, and Japan whose interests are a powerful constraint upon us. If we seriously offend the United States, let us say, by joining the Iron Ore Producers Association, then fear arises: What might the United States do in retaliation?

The point is that Canada is overwhelmingly integrated into the existing world economic system which favours the rich at the expense of the poor. We wish to believe that the system is basically satisfactory, requiring only some slight modification. We wish to believe that by cranking that system up once again the problems of world poverty will be solved or at least will recede. We have not yet reached the point – as a government or society – of recognizing that future reform must essentially favour the poor and thus entail some losses on our part.

Industrial cooperation

The third principal non-aid instrument is industrial cooperation. Here Canada's approach is still foggy because the role of multinational corporations is at the heart of this subject. The industrialization of the developing world requires investment and technology, both of which are primarily available from the private sector, which for the most part means multinational corporations. The spread and growth of multinationals – more accurately called transnationals – is one of the outstanding phenomena of the past two decades. The total value of international production controlled by such corporations now exceeds that of international trade.

The pros and cons of multinationals are hotly debated. In their pursuit of natural resources and markets, in their production of goods and services, in their recruitment and training of employees, in their quest for earnings and distinction, these corporations have succeeded brilliantly in linking capital, technology, materials, and labour from many lands in a creative economic process. On the other hand, transnationals investing in the lesser developed countries tend to control certain sectors of the economy, buying out local enterprises unable to compete with them. There are many cases of US, Japanese, and European transnationals locating plants in Third World countries where wages are low, labour unions weak, tax and general corporation laws advantageous. Consequently, the presence of transnationals in host countries is of principal benefit to the local ruling class, while the real wages of ordinary working people remain at the subsistence level.

90

Canada's position is ambiguous. As a major exporter of mineral resources, largely dominated by US-controlled transnationals, Canada shares an interest with Third World nations that seek to gain control over the development of their natural resources. On the other hand, Canadian-based multinational resource companies, such as Alcan and Falconbridge, have major investments throughout the Third World while Canada remains dependent on the import of many essential raw materials from similar global resource corporations.

Canada is now searching for a model industrial cooperation agreement as a guide to both governments and transnationals. Obviously there ought to be an international legal framework within which transnationals operate; this would be a positive response to the challenge they now present, rather than the negative response of many developing countries that want to nationalize them on the terms of the host country.

Meanwhile, MacEachen told the UN, "We are prepared to make available our own experience in the establishment of screening mechanisms, statistical methods, and techniques of taxation. We support international efforts to enable developing countries to assess their own interests more clearly and to negotiate effectively the terms of the entry of transnational corporations in a manner consistent with their national goals."

The Commonwealth's 'bold action'

The Five-Year Strategy can easily be criticized for being cautiously reformist in character when, in fact, the new economic order demands a radical transfer of wealth and power to the developing world. The Strategy was hardly off the press when GATT-Fly, a team of development experts, sponsored by five Canadian churches, attacked it because it would "only stabilize poverty, not eliminate it." GATT-Fly wanted Canada to adopt "bold measures" to redistribute world economic power.

The Commonwealth Report, produced by a team of ten international experts (Ambassador L. A. H. Smith was the Canadian representative) calls for "bold action" on several fronts that the Canadian government is not yet ready for.

For example, the Commonwealth Report supports indexation and producer associations, both of which Canada thinks would be counter-productive. Commodity prices, in the government's view, have to reflect market forces including the possibilities for substitution by competing products and synthetics. But the Commonwealth Report insists that it is this trend to synthetics that needs immediate attention; it asks for "the imposition of fiscal disincentives on synthetic substitutes in order to ensure that internationally agreed prices for natural products are maintained."

The Commonwealth Report stresses the need for automatic transfer of resources, insisting that Official Development Assistance (ODA) should be raised by all developed countries to 0.7 per cent of GNP immediately and further increased to 1 per cent of GNP by 1980. This, of course is far in excess of what the developed world is providing today; the average is only 0.33 per cent of GNP. The present flow of ODA is inadequate to meet the most pressing problems, let alone support the kind of structural transformation required for a new economic order. This transfer of resources should no longer have the character of "aid," but of "cooperation" in a world-wide effort to mobilize resources for human progress. Then the Commonwealth experts declare: "We consider that the reasons developed countries have advanced in an attempt to explain why annual aid appropriations have failed to allow them to reach the .7 per cent target already . . . have little economic substance or validity."

All that would be required for developed countries to reach 1 per cent by 1980 would be to devote only *5 per cent of the amount by which they will grow richer between 1975 and 1980*. In other words, developed countries could retain 95 per cent of the increase of their GNP and still increase ODA to 1 per cent.

The Canadian government turned this idea down cold. "I am doubtful," said MacEachen, "as to the usefulness of specific targets and dates. At times such dates and targets seem to constitute an impediment rather than a stimulus to positive decisions."

Canada intends to reach the 0.7 per cent figure. But it is the uncertainty of this kind of commitment from developed nations that led the Commonwealth experts to call for an automatic device, such as guaranteeing developing nations a priority on Special Drawing Rights (SDR's), the new form of international currency. If not quite cold, Canada is cool to this idea.

In short, the Commonwealth Report imparts a sense of urgency in implementing "fundamental changes in the world economy, involving a progressive re-distribution of economic activity in favour of the developing countries."Financing is needed on a scale not even envisaged at present for such programs as the arrest of the southward movement of the Sahara Desert in the Sahel area, flood control and protection against typhoons in Bangladesh, rural electrification, and provision of pure water supplies.

Canada's Five-Year Strategy, on the other hand, lacks the sense of urgency that has been the keynote of all the UN conferences on global problems. Still it would be short-sighted to dismiss it because it falls short of the Commonwealth Report and of the New International Economic Order itself. Immediate implementation of the new economic order, as spelled out in UN documents is nearly impossible. It would provoke such economic changes in the West that the backlash would totally undermine public confidence in the work of international development. This is not much comfort to the billion people who can expect little real change in their miserable lives in the rest of this decade. Nonetheless, the only way to offer them substantial hope for the future is to introduce the reforms called for in the new economic order on a step-by-step basis. The giant economic machine of the world is incapable of quick alteration in course, but it can be re-directed, to allow the developing nations to plug into trade and monetary systems, provided the public will to do so is aroused and maintained.

Developing public opinion

A mood of cooperation must dominate new international relationships if there is to be any hope of achieving the new order. The Five-Year Strategy warns that "a hostile reaction by the rich will only intensify the mood of the frustration of the majority of the world's population and foster an atmosphere of confrontation in international affairs."

We are in a dilemma. The massive changes of the new economic order cannot be implemented overnight, the developing world cannot and will not wait for our beneficence to catch up with reality.

One thing is certain: continued reliance on charity is unacceptable. We must set out on a course of justice. Canada must follow a policy that opens the way to change – gradual enough to be accepted domestically, fast enough to be meaningful for the developing world.

This means starting to examine the cost of the new economic order to Canada. Will Canadians pay the price?

When foreign aid meant transferring dollars as a percentage of our GNP, Canadians felt no sacrifice. But now that the full scope of international development is seen to demand a restructuring of the world economy, will Canadians share their standard of living? Or lower it that others might have more? Are we, in short, willing to allocate to developing countries the bulk of our growth in wealth?

These are the kinds of questions that force us to consider the long-range implications of the new order. It is easy enough to give a moral answer and say of course Canadians should accept these sacrificial measures. But in the real world of politics, moralizing does not become action without an intensive program to develop public opinion. And when the public begins to focus on these issues, they will want some guarantees that the benefits of the new order are truly being felt by the poorest people – a guarantee that no government can yet provide because of the terrible complexities of commodity agreements, the impact of

94

transnationals, and internal mechanisms in the developing countries that seem to protect their own elites.

Then, too, Canadians will come up against the hardest question of all: Does progress for us constitute an ever-increasing percentage of production and consumption, while progress for the developing nations means providing only the minimum human requirements of life?

Given the limits to resources on the planet, I do not think it is possible to implement the new order in any meaningful way without reducing our consumption in the industrialized nations. Our per capita consumption cannot continue on an escalator. It does not follow that our standard of living will be reduced by cutting our consumption. The fact is we consume more than we need. But try selling that to the public at a time when our economy is stagnant, inflation is raging, and unemployment is climbing. No, the adoption of the new economic order by Canadians will not be an easy task.

The Canadian role as international bridge-builder sounds impressive, but the foundations of the bridge will consist of public attitudes, and without changes in present attitudes there will not be any bridge. The last point in the Five-Year Strategy emphasizes the need to involve the whole Canadian community: individuals and voluntary organizations, the governments of the provinces, the several departments of the federal and provincial governments, universities, and the business sector. It is in Canada's interest to maintain a leadership role and the test of that leadership will be getting the Five-Year Strategy off the ground.

PART FOUR: WHAT INDIVIDUALS CAN DO

Chapter 7

Canadians Who Care

In 1963 a group of Calgary businessmen heard a Canadian doctor describe his work of thirty years at an eye hospital in Sompeta, India. From that meeting came Operation Eyesight Universal, a group that raises funds throughout Canada to send to the hospital in Sompeta to assist its efforts in preventing blindness and helping the curably blind.

A youth group of the Vancouver YMCA sold Christmas trees to help people in the Solomon Islands build the Women's Homecraft Training Centre. And three Maritime YMCA groups in Halifax, Moncton, and Saint John have formed an "Atlantic Partnership" with the people of the Dominican Republic to establish a YMCA in Santo Domingo.

Les Frères du Sacré-Coeur of Granby, Quebec have recently expanded their rural development project in the Republic of Mali. Their centre, which concentrates on the raising of pigs, gives agricultural training to young people who wish to return to farming and their villages.

Twelve "learner centres" have been established across Canada, providing books and films and programs for the raising of Canadian awareness about the dimensions of world poverty. Their staffs visit schools and community groups to talk about such things as Canadian trade policy and the Third World, the effects of malnutrition in Africa and Asia, and the need for a new global ethic.

In May 1975 a "Week for the World" was organized in Ottawa by CUSO and Pollution Probe. The program included speeches by Canadian government officials, and by Cesar Chavez and Ralph Nader from the United States. A hunger banquet was held with a menu of homemade vegetable soup and brown bread. The money raised by selling tickets to this feast, meagre by our standards but generous beyond belief for many in the world, went to development projects submitted by Canadian Non Governmental Organizations (NGOs).

What all these projects have in common is that they were originated and developed by private organizations in Canada, groups like CUSO, CARE, and the Canadian Catholic Organization for Development and Peace, the Mennonite Central Committee, Oxfam, and the Canadian Save the Children Fund. Throughout Canada there are hundreds of such groups run by young and not-so-young Canadians having one central purpose in mind – to bring the immense poverty of the world into the minds and imaginations of Canadians and to bring some of our wealth and commitment to bear on the elimination of that poverty. NGOs provide striking testimony that there are many Canadians who care about the state of the world and have enough personal initiative to do something about it.

Every shape and size

The NGOs are of every shape, size, and philosophy. Some like CARE or OXFAM are well-known large organizations which rival governments in their expertise. Others are tiny and yet highly effective. Some like CUSO send Canadians to live and work in every part of the developing world under conditions very different from the comfort back home. Some send money. Their philosophies vary: some stress charity; others radical political change. Their common bond is an underlying awareness of the tragic difference between the rich and poor of the world.

The Churches of Canada have been an important instrument in the "consciousness-raising" of Canadians. Historically, missionaries are thought of as bearers of the gospel among the developing countries. What is less understood is that missionaries were among the first to realize that people do not welcome the gospel on an empty stomach, and that even if you distribute bread you are only dealing with the effect, not the cause, of mass poverty.

Gradually, missionaries, both ordained and lay, began to blend their activities as preachers, healers, and agents of social change. This does not mean that the Churches – taken as a whole – have thrust themselves into the development question. They have not. The Churches have been preoccupied with preaching the good news of salvation, which many adherents maintain is their principal responsibility. It would take me too far afield here to discuss all the reasons why the development efforts of the Churches have been modest. I merely want to emphasize that while the Churches ought to have done much more through the years to awaken people at home and abroad to the need for social change in keeping with the dignity of man as a spiritual creature – at the same time within the Churches are found dynamic people and movements who are in the vanguard of thought and action on the development front.

This range of activity comes into sharp focus in the annual Ten Days for World Development Program and the year-round efforts of GATT-Fly.

Ten Days for World Development is a joint development education program of the Anglican, Catholic, Lutheran, Presbyterian, and United Churches of Canada. For ten days during Lent, the program sends Church leaders across the country, presents briefs to the government, initiates media events, and stimulates follow-up programs in local communities. The program has made a lot of headway, but the organizers note, realistically: "There are many obstacles to be overcome before it can be honestly said that there is a groundswell movement of international concern in Canada." The coordinator of the program (Robert Gardner, 600 Jarvis Street, Room 219, Toronto) provides a wide range of up-to-date films, books, and pamphlets for general use.

GATT-Fly is a team of young experts, sponsored by the same five Churches and the Canadian Council of Churches, working year-round to stimulate public concern for a Canadian trade and monetary policy in line with the new economic order. The name conveys the idea of a fly buzzing around and bothering the moguls of the General Agreement on Trades and Tariffs that for too long has protected the interest of the rich countries at the expense of the poor. GATT-Fly members turn up at the big international conferences, prodding Canadian officials to take stronger stands in support of developing countries.

GATT-Fly is chiefly a critic of government policy, a necessary function since there is so little informed criticism of Canada's international work. It is therefore highly specialized. The work of the various Church agencies is more general and easier for people to relate to.

The Canadian Catholic Organization for Development and Peace, 67 Bond Street, Toronto, was begun by the Catholic bishops as the development arm of the Church, quite distinct from traditional missionary activity. It provides funds to be administered by developing peoples in programs of their own design. Currently more than $4 million a year is dispensed out of Lenten collections.

In the United Church of Canada, the Division of World Outreach, 85 St. Clair Avenue East, Toronto, sends personnel abroad to work under the direction of national Churches in about twenty countries. These Canadians work in a wide range of fields: education, hospitals, village clinics, child care, agriculture, cooperatives, adult education, radio, audio-visuals. United Church personnel also work with oecumenical bodies. For example, the United Church shares in the support of an agriculturalist from the Methodist Church of Brazil serving with the Methodist Church of Angola.

Canadian Lutheran World Relief, 1820 Arlington Street,

Winnipeg, began as an effort to supply food, clothing, and relief to refugees in war-torn Europe. Since then it has evolved into a world-wide program of relief and development which has dispensed nearly $9 million in funds and gifts to twenty-three poor countries. Its current program "To Help a Broken World" is aimed at alleviating the world food crisis.

The Committee on Inter-Church Aid Refugee and World Service of the Presbyterian Church of Canada, 50 Wynford Drive, Don Mills, Ontario, has assisted in providing emergency aid in such disasters as a recent Mexican earthquake, the Sahelian drought, and refugee resettlement in Cyprus. Following such disasters further development assistance is provided to help people get back on their feet again. For example, in Bangladesh as refugees returned from the civil war, help was extended in establishing new housing units, and in providing seed, fertilizer, and farm equipment.

Similar projects are supported by the Primate's World Relief Fund of the Anglican Church, 600 Jarvis Street, Toronto, which has maintained an emphasis on overseas work.

While the Churches have been in the forefront of Canadian development efforts, they are by no means the only major NGOs. Let us look at some of the others.

CUSO – Canadian University Service Overseas
151 Slater Street, Ottawa

The idea of having university graduates devote a year or two of their lives to working in a developing country first found expression, and enormous popularity, in the United States Peace Corps. This latter seemed a perfect way for idealistic young people to make a tangible contribution and to experience how others live at the same time. Out of this basic idea and fervour there developed similar organizations throughout the rich world, including CUSO in Canada.

CUSO was formed in 1961 as an association of university groups interested in overseas service. In that year the first group of fifteen volunteers left for one year assignments in India and

Ceylon. Since then some 6,000 volunteers have served in over forty countries and today there are 825 workers in Africa, the Caribbean, and Latin America. Over the years the largest single CUSO program has been in education. For example, in Nigeria the government is using its new oil wealth to achieve Universal Primary Education and CUSO provides a large contingent of teachers. In Jamaica, CUSO and the Ministry of Education are in the fifth year of a remedial reading program.

In addition to education, CUSO has volunteers working in primary health care. Typical of these is a public health nurse in Ghana responsible for maternal and child care services in a large, remote rural area. And recently CUSO, in common with many development organizations has placed increased emphasis on agricultural assistance. In the tiny country of Belize in Central America, CUSO provided a government forester, a home economist to work on home canning techniques with rural women, and a co-op manager as part of a large cooperatives project.

A distinctive feature of CUSO operations is that volunteers are paid at local wage rates and at least partly by the host governments. In this way the enormous gap between the "wealthy foreigner" and the local people is reduced and it is ensured that the volunteer is genuinely wanted. This system guarantees an unusual degree of motivation.

The story of CUSO is essentially the stories of thousands of individual volunteers. John Davies, a pharmacist in Burnaby, British Columbia, was a bit bored. "I was looking for a job with some excitement, some variety." He found it as the chief dispenser of drugs in a hospital in St. Lucia. The job involves management, purchasing, and teaching. "The good aspects of the job are not hard to find. There's a basic challenge I enjoy."

Lena Swee Sim Tan is an economics graduate from the University of British Columbia who, "in the absence of anyone else who can teach these subjects," is head of the physics and math departments at a girls' secondary school in Bakana, Nigeria. She finds that many of the students have difficulty in class.

"One problem is poor nutrition and poor health . . . The school diet is generally starchy and monotonous, for example, tea and bread for breakfast. Most of them have had malaria. When there is no electricity, they study by dim kerosene lamp or candles."

CESO – Canadian Executive Service Overseas
Suite 420, 1010 St. Catherine St., W., Montreal

CESO is an organization run by retired Canadian businessmen to provide executive and professional people for projects in developing countries. Volunteers serve for a maximum of six months in response to specific requests from organizations abroad. CESO in turn maintains a file of volunteers' qualifications which it attempts to make known abroad. No salary is paid to these volunteers, unless, as it frequently is, by their own company. CESO pays transportation and the host organization provides accommodation and living and work expenses. More than 1,000 Canadians have so far served in some forty countries.

CESO provides help either to private or government enterprises in the form of technical or managerial guidance such as making a feasibility study, "tuning up" an existing operation or assisting with training programs. In recruiting its volunteers CESO stressed the crucial importance of sensitivity to local society. "It is important for both the man and his wife to be understanding about the politics, traditions, institutions, attitudes and religious practices existing in the country. Usually they are not better or worse than ours – merely different and frequently much older."

CANSAVE – Canadian Save the Children Fund
70 Hayter St., Toronto

The Canadian Save the Children Fund is affiliated with the International Union for Child Welfare, founded in the United Kingdom in 1919. Its work is based on the ideals of the UN

Declaration of the Rights of the Child, the preamble to which reads simply: "Mankind owes the child the best it has to give."

The Union for Child Welfare was founded to help in a specific situation – the starvation and homelessness of millions of children during the Russian Civil wars. Fifty years later, relief efforts are still an important part of CANSAVE's job but in addition it now directs its efforts to changing those conditions that "make our help necessary in the first place."

A current project is the Child Welfare Training Centre in Kingston, St. Vincent in the Windward Islands. Most Canadians reclining on the beaches of the luxurious tourist hotels in the Caribbean never see the poverty around them. In the Windward Chain of islands there is widespread malnutrition and high infant mortality. The Training Centre tries to alleviate this suffering by bringing students from throughout the Caribbean to learn the fundamentals of nutrition, sanitation, and early child care. After a year's training the students return to local centres where they work with mothers and school teachers.

Another CANSAVE project is the sponsoring of a group of boys at Boys Town in Costa Rica. Here orphaned boys – and there are countless orphans throughout the developing world – are given a home and taught woodworking, tailoring, metal crafts, baking, and other skills which help support the institution and prepare the boys for careers at the same time.

Oxfam-Canada
175 Carlton St., Toronto

Oxfam derives its name from the Oxford Committee for Famine Relief founded in Britain during World War II to help civilians suffering from severe famine in Greece. This effort, controversial because it involved sending supplies through a British blocade of Nazi-occupied Europe, set the pattern for Oxfam involvement in disasters everywhere in the developing world. In recent years it has been active in "drought-stricken Africa, disaster-prone Bangladesh and war-torn Biafra." Its emphasis has been put increasingly upon helping the poor in the developing world, for "grinding poverty is a kind of never-ending disaster."

In its development programs, Oxfam has helped with literacy, education and vocational training, in agriculture, water-supply and health, in family planning, and producer cooperatives. In providing this help, Oxfam stresses "human self-realization" by seeking maximum local participation in the planning and carrying out of projects.

These are only a few of the more than 100 NGOs in Canada, most of whom are affiliated with the Canadian Council for International Cooperation, 75 Sparks Street, Ottawa. The wide variety of NGOs suggests many ways in which any Canadian anywhere can make contact with the work of world economic justice.

Raising money

As we have seen, Canadian NGOs are involved in far more than just fund raising for development. They provide as well a large supply of human skills to assist developing countries. And yet in development as in everything else money remains essential.

Over the years NGOs have raised hundreds of millions of dollars in Canada. The individual donation of 5 or 10 dollars is the most familiar form of fund raising but NGOs have shown great ingenuity in developing other techniques as well. Miles for Millions was organized by Oxfam as a way for Canadians to participate while contributing. Canadian businesses are canvassed regularly to provide money and materials.

In fact, stimulating the involvement of Canadians is at the heart of two growing programs, matching funds and development education.

CIDA's Public Participation Program makes grants to projects sponsored by NGOs on a matching basis – which means that CIDA contributes up to 50 per cent of the total project cost. Thus NGOs are encouraged to raise private funds for projects overseas, knowing that every dollar they raise is worth two dollars. As far as the private donor is concerned, the first dollar is tax deductible and the second dollar comes out of his taxes. From CIDA's point of view, this method greatly increases the total Canadian aid sent overseas.

In 1973-74, the $21 million provided by CIDA in matching grants generated an additional flow of $45 million in development assistance in cash, goods and services from the private sector. In this way 654 projects worth $66 million were funded in eighty-nine countries.

CIDA, of course, must approve the projects but more experimentation and flexibility is allowed than in projects funded totally by government. A senior official of CIDA, Lewis Perinbam, maintains that many NGOs are well ahead of governments in international development cooperation. "Indeed, we are happy that they are there to pace us and to provide an incentive to our efforts."

The matching grant system is now spreading into the provinces. In 1973, Alberta led the way by inaugurating a plan that quadrupled development dollars raised in that province. Alberta agrees to match each dollar raised by an Alberta NGO – up to a $2 million limit. The $4 million is then matched by CIDA, providing $8 million for overseas projects. In the first full year forty-seven projects were funded, including a Day Care Community Centre in Turkey, a rapeseed project in Peru, and a mobile health service in Ghana. Many NGOs find they are able to raise more money through the stimulus of the matching grant. For example, Operation Eyesight Universal, mentioned at the beginning of this chapter, raised $35,240 in 1973 – 74. When matching grants came into effect the next year, the organization raised $73,503.

Raising public consciousness

Nobody knows better than NGOs how much development education is needed among Canadians – to raise their consciousness about world conditions. Consequently an increasing amount of NGO activity is concentrated on education programs aimed at helping Canadians understand the new economic order. After all, what good does it do to squeeze money out of people while they eat, drive, and generally consume in ways that just add to the problem?

In discussing the various NGOs we have described such educational efforts as Ten Days for World Development and GATT-Fly. The essential purpose of such activities is to help Canadians see the contrast – and the connection – between their way of life and the suffering of millions of poor throughout the world. The object is not to denounce righteously but to see ourselves from another angle, "as others see us." In the words of a recent Ten Days publication "the fact remains that, compared to the overwhelming majority of the inhabitants of this planet, Canadians generally can be fairly described as having great possessions."

In striving to educate, NGOs make every effort to reach Canadians where they live, drawing upon the resources and experiences of the local community.

The Alberta Committee of International Cooperation has proven that an intensive program can excite and energize a whole community. For six weeks in the fall of 1975 it ran a World Reflections program throughout the province that had the character of a festival – with exhibits, cultural shows, TV specials, workshops and school visits. It took a year-and-a-half of planning, $60,000, the cooperation of art galleries, the CBC, libraries, museums, the National Film Board, provincial government, Churches, school boards, service clubs, theatre groups, and universities – and out of it all came a way to present global issues in a challenging, positive way.

And yet one must not expect that educating ourselves to the realities of the world will always be such a "pleasant" experience. Development education leaders have often found themselves on thin ice. People and governments will give money to organizations that feed the hungry and nurse the sick. But when these organizations turn up as allies to radical groups who want to overthrow corrupt governments in developing countries, or when they pressure the Canadian government to move into trade and monetary changes it isn't ready for – that raises hackles. Most NGOs are very cautious, recognizing that they operate at the good will of the public and the government. The fear of going too fast has checked development education efforts.

As we move into the new era in development we must consider whether Canadians can demand only comforting words and "practical advice" from those who have seen the world and fear for its future. In talking about the difference between practical politics and the role of NGOs one of the committed young people in GATT-Fly referred to the "prophetic voice." It is not a soothing voice. It is not a complacent voice. It will not tell us what so many would like to hear, that if only we do more of the same all will be well. Prophecy is impatient and critical. It is not full of excuses for the way things are.

Chapter 8

45 Things You Can Do

A big subject, development.

Big problems, big government decisions, big organizations.

It seems too much for one person to do anything about.

Not at all. In fact the way to get big plans rolling is for individuals to take small steps. Walt Whitman put this movingly:

"Even for the treatment of the universal, in politics, metaphysics, or anything, sooner or later we come down to one single, solitary soul."

And now we're down to you and me.

Here's a list of things we can do – and it wasn't hard to reach forty-five. There are never any perfect places to start – only real ones.

1. Put up a picture of Julius Nyerere or Dom Helder Camara in your house. Have your children find out who they are.

2. Skip a meal once a week or once a month to increase your awareness of hunger. Or try a Fourth World diet for a day. Little or no food.

3. Think "necessity" when you buy. If you don't need that dish washer why buy it?

4. Phone a hot-line radio show when they are discussing a

subject that could be related to world development. Raise the level of community concern.

5. Write a letter to the Prime Minister asking for a copy of his speech on a new ethic of sharing given at the Mansion House, London, England. (Can you imagine the reaction in the East Block if every voter did this?)

6. Write to your M.P. asking what he or she is doing to implement Canada's New Five-Year Strategy for International Development Cooperation. (There's a trick to writing M.P.s. You'll always get a response to your letter, probably composed by his secretary. Write a second time. This forces the M.P. to start taking you seriously. What can you lose? It doesn't even cost you a stamp.)

7. Buy UNICEF Christmas cards, and speaking of Christmas, the Alternate Christmas Catalogue will give you a whole new perspective on Christmas-giving.

8. Do you have immigrants from developing countries living in your community? Invite one to dinner in your home and ask about life in his country.

9. If you are a doctor, consider a sabbatical to work in Asia or Africa for a year; if you're a farmer find out what Canadian agricultural methods are needed in the developing world; if you're a university student, do a term paper on Falconbridge Mines in Namibia.

10. If you're thinking about adoption, consider international adoption. Your Children's Aid Society can help you.

11. Put a developing world money box on the kitchen table for family donations. But don't do it unless you sit the family down for a chat about consumption habits. Try to help them see that eating less meat and drinking less beer and liquor will have the long-term effect of freeing grain for direct consumption by those who need it.

12. Set a place at dinner every night for your "unseen guest" from the Fourth World. It will be a daily reminder of the millions we don't want to be reminded of.

13. Quit smoking and put the money in the kitchen table money box. (I admit this one may be too tough.)

14. Invite someone from the developing world to your church. A guest sermon on Christianity in the West Indies might open a lot of eyes.

15. Stop fertilizing your lawn – or at least do it less often. Cutting down on fertilizer for non-food purposes will free more of it for growing food.

16. Be an energy miser. So canoe rather than putt-putt, cross-country ski rather than downhill, walk don't drive.

17. Disapprove of snowmobiles (politely).

18. At the next election campaign, stand up at the all-candidates meetings and ask for commitments to support world development. And don't accept vague answers from politicians.

19. Organize a club, church, or community evening on the topic "What World Development Means to Me." Start with a supper. When the people arrive sit them at tables of four. Give one person at each table a super dinner of steak, mashed potatoes, green beans and salad, hot rolls, wine, apple pie with ice cream and coffee. Give the other three a small quantity of watery soup and a stale piece of bread. Allow no substitutions and let anybody leave who wants to. You won't have to worry about the discussion being stimulating.

20. Find out who Mother Teresa is.

21. If you're a teacher, assign your class to research the local paper for stories in the past year on the New International Economic Order, and do the same thing for stories on Patty Hearst.

22. If you're not a teacher, take my word for it that the ratio is about 1 – 25. Write to the editor of your local paper and tell him that if he's downplaying news articles about the New Economic Order because he thinks you aren't interested, he's making a big mistake.

23. Ask the National Film Board for a film on the role of women in the developing world. Put on a screening but try to

get some men present as well as women so they can see the intolerable conditions most women in the world are subjected to.

24. Get more information on development. Write CIDA and ask for their monthly magazine on development, *Cooperation Canada*. It's lively, well-written and very enlightening.

25. Adopt an NGO. Get to know people in the Learner Centre nearest you. You'll find a dozen ways you can help them, beginning by offering them a meal at your house.

26. There's nothing wrong with giving money. Give it to an NGO for a project so that your dollar – through matching grants – could become two or four dollars, depending on where you live.

27. If you live in a province that doesn't yet have matching grants, write to your Premier and ask him to pitch in. If your province does this, tell your Premier he's on the ball.

28. Promote and organize an oecumenical study-action group in your community with a fixed number of meetings. Use material from GATT-Fly or Ten Days for World Development to help the group see how common religious values about human life and human dignity can deepen awareness of social issues. Invite your local M.P. to your last meeting, and have it when he can guarantee his presence. Then tell him what you've learned.

29. Are you about to graduate from university with a medical, educational, or technical skill? How about spending the first two years of your career in a developing country? CUSO will tell you how.

30. Develop a healthy sense of outrage about a so-called civilization that permits such massive and needless suffering in the world – and that spends twenty-six times as much on armaments – as on human development.

31. There's a growing list of solid readable books on the development question. Here are just three – any one of which could change your life if you take it seriously.

Mankind at the Turning Point
By Mihajlo Mesarovic and Eduard Pestel

E. P. Dutton and Co. Inc./Reader's Digest Press
New York 1974

New Hope for the Hungry?
By Larry Minear
Friendship Press, New York

Small is Beautiful: A Study of Economics as if People Mattered
By E. F. Schumacher
Abacus Paperbacks (Canadian distributor: Thomas Nelson & Sons, Ltd., Toronto)

32. Don't fall into the "Afghanistan" trap – safely criticizing something far away. What about our own native people? Many of them are excluded from true development also. And what about destitute pensioners in our own community? A fully developed sense of justice knows no boundaries.

33. If you work in the textile or footwear industries, ask your union to organize a meeting to explore the future of these industries, related to the New Economic Order.

34. Get your children to put together a photo montage of children throughout the world. Help them to understand the difference between being born in Canada and the Punjab. While you're at it, check how much about the developing world they're learning in school.

35. Instead of the latest rock hit, put on a record of the music of Africa. See how the family reacts.

36. Sponsor a foster child through the Foster Parents Plan. Make sure everyone in the family writes to the child.

37. Write the Presidents of the CBC and CTV asking couldn't they please put on prime time some of the world development documentaries their staffs are perfectly capable of producing – instead of such a relentless procession of sitcoms, medical adventures, and detective stories.

38. There's probably a cable TV station near you. It needs good community programming (or it will forfeit its license). Organize

a group and talk to the manager about using his station to involve your community in development.

39. Participate in international student exchange programs.

40. Ask your priest, minister, or rabbi to preach next week on the role of religion in the New International Economic Order.

41. Support Miles for Millions. Sponsor a child, anyone, in the next walkathon, swimathon, bikeathon, or skateathon.

42. Bring the suffering of victims of war and hunger into your prayers before meals.

43. Tax yourself 5 per cent of your income and give it to a United Nations agency working in the development field. Of course this is voluntary, but you'll be in the advance wing of what must come inevitably – a mandatory world tax.

44. Get involved in politics at the grass roots level. Any constituency organization will welcome you, especially if you're willing to work. Only the concerted efforts of politically conscious people will make the world development issues part of the party platforms and eventually legislative action.

45. Stop. Ask yourself: Am I part of the solution or part of the problem?

And remember the ancient Roman scholar, Pliny, who wrote, How many things are considered impossible until they are actually done!"

Morality and Politics: A Common Front

A fascinating occurrence marks this moment in history. For a long time philosophers, theologians, and others with strong moral convictions have insisted that a society based on escalating consumer consumption for its economic success will eventually self-destruct. Such a system so "over-develops" the privileged that it actually dims our sense of social justice and weakens the moral fibres of compassion, concern, and commitment to the disadvantaged.

A preoccupation with increasing our own comfort and wealth distorts our sense of values and flies in the face of the great moral teachings that religion has transmitted through the ages. But this, of course, is a religionless age. Or so it would seem to a visitor from outer space trying to comprehend how a civilization that prides itself on technological accomplishment can be so impervious to the call of our brothers for bread and opportunity.

The argument that a civilization directed to increasing material improvement is unable to satisfy the human spirit has been regarded as some kind of poetry. Pleas for social justice, domestically and internationally, have attracted but a handful of adherents. Statements that the quantity of life syndrome should

117

be replaced by the quality of life ethic have been put off as philosophies to be approached gradually, The business of the day, politics as usual, must go on because, after all, growth is the standard and band-aids the remedy for breakdowns.

Now, however, thanks to the new global crises we have suddenly come up against a hitherto inconceivable prospect: maybe unlimited consumerism will have to come to an end. Maybe the rich of the world have over-reached themselves. Maybe a whole new assessment of how we live will have to be made. Exactly.

That is the message of the new economic order.

The new order, based on the expertise of an international array of political, scientific, and technical leaders, was arrived at through perceiving massive global disorder. The ecologists know that famine is technologically unnecessary. The political scientists can observe the rise of warring tensions over the rich-poor gap.

Thus, from two different streams of life – the moral and the pragmatic – there is a convergence on a common goal: a better system of sharing as stewards of the planet. This convergence – for the first time since the evolution of the modern world – is what gives me hope in an age that is still marked by frustration, despair, and violence. It is a powerful convergence because it now makes possible a new global ethic.

A new global ethic is the moral expression of concern for the well-being of our neighbours on the planet. But it is also a political imperative if there is to be any stability, security, and peace on the planet. Spiritual values and physical dangers have created a juxtaposition of philosophical and political realities. The new economic order responds to the call of the humanists for justice. Viewed as an old ethic or a new order, what is now being commonly promoted is a system that would ensure minimum economic standards for every human being.

The new global ethic, in short, is this: that there would be enough food, shelter, and clothing for every human being on earth along with the opportunity to live in self-fulfilment. That

118

is the minimum to protect human dignity and decency. Anything else is declaring bankruptcy in our society. Answers to these problems, maintains Prime Minister Michael Manley of Jamaica "will be found within the framework of a perceived global ethic, whether arrived at by a moral or pragmatic route."

The new global ethic is primarily an attitude toward the integrity of the human person and the harmony of organic growth. It is also the only practical response to societal breakdown. I believe immense gains can now be made by recognition that what has always been good for the soul is now urgent for the body.

Thus, this new common front of religion and politics must be grasped to alter our course – even at this late hour – from the path of disorder. The crisis has given birth to a new opportunity. The mood of self-doubt can give way to self-confidence.

A precondition for the new global ethic is the development of a world consciousness. Obviously this must be inculcated in the generation now in school. But we cannot wait until today's youngsters enter positions of leadership. It is the work of politics and religion to help the generation still in charge in the last quarter of this century to get a vision of social justice, of the interdependence of all mankind. Unless the equality, the oneness, and the common dignity of mankind pervade the vision, then violence and terrorism will sweep the world.

Here the role of religion, in awakening us to the spiritual qualities that bind mankind, is especially important. It is, after all, the fundamental teaching of the Scriptures that we are our brother's keeper and that, if we leave the least of our fellow men to misery, hunger, and early death, "the blood of Abel will call from the ground" for judgement and brand us with the mark of Cain. It takes great energy and fortitude to undo the injustices of centuries and to rise above the ease of comfort and success. But unless we insist on sharing the blessings of the planet, we will surely die inwardly from lack of moral purpose.

Religion is often identified with charity. In the sense that charity means love, it is a proper identification. But in the sense that charity means alms, or the giving of some small surplus to the needy, it is an identification that misses the wholeness of life and is, moreover, hopelessly overtaken by events. The waging of war on misery requires far more than charity; it demands an enlarged concept of justice. Peace is not just the absence of war, it is something that is built up day after day, in the pursuit of an order intended by God, which implies a more perfect form of justice among peoples.

In short, charity, as we have been practising it, is satisfying all our desires and then passing on some of what is left over; justice requires adjusting our desires to the needs of others, so that there is a planetary sharing of what all have a right to. The fiery Brazilian crusader Dom Helder Camara puts the case for development well: "When shall we have the courage to outgrow the charity mentality and see that at the bottom of all relations between rich and poor there is the problem of justice?"

The voice of religion, demanding justice for the dispossessed and disadvantaged of the world, must now cut through the din and clamour of a confused age. Nothing is challenged more than religion to help create the kind of future community which is the goal of the new economic order. The crises of our time are challenging the world religions to release a new spiritual force transcending religious, cultural, and national boundaries. This means that religions must speak together, utilizing the deep spiritual resources found in the diverse religious traditions of mankind.

The World Conference on Religion for Peace (WCRP), bringing together Christians, Jews, Muslims, Hindus, and Buddhists, provides an example of how religions can work together for the cause of peace and justice. I attended WCRP's Second World Conference at the Louvain, Belgium, in 1974 and became convinced that religion could be heard on global issues if it genuinely attempted to speak with one voice. "We appeal to the religious communities of the world," WCRP declared, "to inculcate the attitude of planetary citizenship, the sense of our human solidarity in the just sharing of the food, the energy, and all the material necessities which our generous habitat, unlike any other yet perceived in universal space, will continue faithfully to provide if only it is well loved and respected by mankind."

The role of leadership today is to live and teach this new global ethic and to impart a sense of hope that the world economic structure can be radically altered.

Tables

The First World

Country	Pop. (000)	GNP (1972) Amount (US $ millions)	GNP (1972) Per Cap. (US $)	Growth Rates % Pop. 1965 – 72	Growth Rates % GNP Per Cap. 1965 – 72
Australia	12,960	38,660	2,980	1.9	3.1
Austria	7,490	18,090	2,410	0.4	5.0
Belgium	9,710	31,200	3,210	0.3	4.6
Canada	21,850	97,080	4,440	1.5	3.2
Denmark	4,990	18,330	3,670	0.7	3.7
Finland	4,630	13,000	2,810	0.2	4.9
France	51,720	187,360	3,620	0.8	4.8
Iceland	207	580	2,800	1.0	1.8
Ireland	3,010	4,760	1,580	0.6	3.7
Italy	54,350	106,660	1,960	0.6	4.3
Japan	106,960	247,890	2,320	1.1	9.7
Luxemburg	350	1,120	3,190	0.6	3.0
Netherlands	13,330	37,910	2,840	1.2	4.3
New Zealand	2,900	7,420	2,560	1.3	1.8
Norway	3,930	13,140	3,340	0.8	3.8
Portugal	9,803	7,610	780	0.9	5.3
Spain	34,369	41,470	1,210	1.1	5.0
South Africa	23,650	20,050	850	3.3	2.1
Sweden	8,120	36,350	4,480	0.7	2.5
Switzerland	6,280	24,720	3,940	1.0	2.9
United Kingdom	55,800	144,900	2,600	0.4	2.0
United States	208,840	1,167,420	5,590	1.0	2.0
West Germany	61,670	208,970	3,390	0.6	4.1

The details in these tables are World Bank figures for 1972, reported in the 1974 World Bank Atlas.

The Second World

Country	Pop. (000)	GNP (1972) Amount (US $ millions)	GNP (1972) Per Cap. (US $)	Growth Rates % Pop. 1965 – 72	Growth Rates % GNP Per Cap. 1965 – 72
Albania	2,255	1,190	530	2.7	5.7
Bulgaria	8,579	12,190	1,420	0.6	5.9
China	786,440	133,700	170	1.8	2.6
Cuba	8,750	3,970	450	1.8	– 1.0
Czechoslovakia	14,481	31,580	2,180	0.3	4.5
East Germany	17,043	35,740	2,100	0.0	3.5
Hungary	10,398	15,860	1,520	0.3	4.2
Mongolia	1,319	510	380	2.7	0.6
North Korea	14,680	4,730	320	2.8	4.0
North Vietnam	22,040	2,310	110	2.1	– 0.1
Poland	33,068	49,640	1,500	0.8	4.0
Romania	20,700	16,770	810	1.3	6.7
South Vietnam	19,300	3,300	170	2.6	– 0.7
U.S.S.R.	247,460	377,700	1,530	1.0	5.9

The Third World

Country	Pop: (000)	GNP (1972) Amount (US $ millions)	Per Cap. (US $)	Growth Rates % Pop. 1965-72	GNP Per Cap 1965-72
Algeria*	14,260	6,120	430	3.5	3.5
Argentina	23,946	30,970	1,290	1.6	2.8
Barbados	239	190	800	0.3	6.2
Bolivia	5,194	1,030	200	2.6	1.4
Botswana	629	150	240	1.9	10.0
Brazil	98,203	52,010	530	2.9	5.6
Cameroon	6,084	1,230	200	1.9	3.8
Chile	10,040	8,030	800	2.1	2.2
Colombia	23,039	9,270	400	3.2	2.4
Congo, People's Republic of	1,151	340	300	2.2	1.4
Costa Rica	1,823	1,150	630	2.9	4.1
Cyprus	650	760	1,180	1.2	6.4
Dominican Rep.	4,234	1,980	480	2.6	5.0
Ecuador*	6,514	2,370	360	3.4	3.8
Egypt	34,840	8,340	240	2.5	0.6
El Salvador	3,665	1,250	340	3.3	1.2
Equatorial Guinea	301	70	240	1.7	-1.5
Fiji	541	270	500	2.3	4.9
Gabon*	494	440	880	1.0	10.0
Ghana	9,086	2,700	300	2.6	1.0
Greece	8,940	13,020	1,460	0.6	7.3
Guatemala	5,623	2,340	420	3.4	2.2
Guinea-Bissau	568	130	230	0.9	3.4
Guyana	754	300	400	2.4	1.3
Honduras	2,687	860	320	2.9	1.7
Indonesia*	121,630	10,940	90	2.1	4.3
Iran*	31,169	15,220	490	3.2	7.2
Iraq*	10,070	3,730	370	3.3	1.8
Israel	3,080	8,050	2,610	2.7	7.1
Ivory Coast	5,400	1,840	340	3.3	4.1
Jamaica	1,931	1,560	810	1.3	3.9
Jordan	2,470	670	270	3.5	-2.8
Kuwait*	840	3,440	4,090	8.7	-1.3
Lebanon	2,891	2,030	700	2.7	1.4
Liberia	1,617	410	250	3.1	4.0

The Third World Continued

Country	Pop. (000)	GNP (1972)		Growth Rates %	
		Amount (US $ millions)	Per Cap. (US $)	Pop. 1965–72	GNP Per Cap. 1965–72
Libyan Arab Rep.*	2,084	3,820	1,830	3.7	8.1
Malaysia	11,450	4,930	430	2.8	2.9
Malta	320	300	950	0.4	7.4
Mauritius	849	250	300	-1.6	0.0
Mexico	54,152	40,340	750	3.5	2.8
Morocco	15,840	4,260	270	2.5	3.0
Mozambique	7,962	2,400	300	2.0	5.6
Nicaragua	2,152	1,020	470	3.0	1.5
Nigeria*	69,524	9,350	130	2.5	5.4
Panama	1,524	1,340	880	3.1	4.5
Papua New Guinea	2,581	750	290	2.8	7.5
Paraguay	2,354	740	320	2.5	2.1
Peru	14,122	7,380	520	2.8	1.1
Philipines	39,040	8,620	220	3.0	2.4
Qatar	130	330	2,530	8.8	6.1
Rhodesia	5,690	1,920	340	3.5	2.9
Saudi Arabia*	7,616	4,160	550	1.7	6.8
Senegal	3,990	1,050	260	2.2	− 0.7
Singapore	2,147	2,790	1,300	1.8	10.3
South Korea	32,360	9,880	310	1.9	8.5
Swaziland	446	120	260	3.0	5.3
Syrian Arab Rep.	6,740	2,150	320	3.3	3.8
Taiwan	15,130	7,400	490	2.9	6.9
Thailand	38,498	8,340	220	3.1	4.2
Trinidad and Tobago	1,048	1,020	970	0.9	3.6
Tunisia	5,340	2,040	380	3.0	3.7
Turkey	37,010	13,650	370	2.4	4.3
United Arab Emirates	257	830	3,220	9.3	16.2
Uruguay	2,959	2,240	760	1.2	0.4
Venezuela*	11,108	13,820	1,240	3.6	1.1
Yugoslavia	20,772	16,790	810	0.9	5.5
Zambia	4,515	1,730	380	2.9	− 0.1

*denotes a petroleum exporter. Therefore the GNP and GNP per capita are now substantially higher than 1972 because of the rapid increase in oil prices.

The Fourth World

Country	Pop. (000)	GNP (1972)		Growth Rates %	
		Amount (US % millions)	Per Cap. (US $)	Pop. 1965-72	GNP Per Cap. 1965-72
Afghanistan	14,878	1,220	80	2.0	0.8
Bangladesh	72,500	4,750	70	2.5	-1.6
Bhutan	933	70	80	1.7	0.4
Burma	28,874	2,580	90	2.2	1.0
Burundi	3,506	230	70	2.0	1.1
Central African Rep.	1,673	260	160	2.2	2.3
Chad	3,780	320	80	1.8	1.6
Dahomey	2,860	300	110	2.8	1.7
Ethiopia	25,930	2,140	80	2.4	1.2
Gambia	377	50	140	1.9	1.4
Guinea	5,100	440	90	2.8	-0.3
Haiti	4,377	560	130	1.6	1.3
India	563,490	61,940	110	2.3	1.4
Kenya	12,070	2,050	170	3.3	4.1
Lesotho	959	80	90	2.0	1.1
Malagasy Rep.	7,400	1,030	140	2.5	1.4
Malawi	4,711	460	100	2.6	2.9
Mali	5,260	400	80	2.1	1.3
Mauritania	1,210	210	180	1.9	2.0
Nepal	11,470	950	80	1.8	0.1
Niger	4,250	400	90	2.8	-5.1
Pakistan	66,720	8,800	130	4.1	1.7
Rwanda	3,904	250	60	3.2	2.1
Sierre Leone	2,727	520	190	2.2	1.8
Somalia	2,964	240	80	2.5	1.1
Sri Lanka	13,198	1,390	110	2.3	2.0
Sudan	16,586	2,030	120	2.8	-1.1
Tanzania	13,606	1,580	120	2.8	2.9
Togo	2,052	330	160	2.7	3.3
Uganda	10,479	1,560	150	2.9	2.0
Upper Volta	5,613	400	70	2.1	0.6
Western Samoa	150	20	150	2.4	0.4
Yemen Arab Rep.	6,060	550	90	2.2	2.4
Yemen, People's Rep. of	1,510	150	100	2.9	-7.2
Zaire	19,091	1,920	100	2.6	3.9

Acknowledgements

I am indebted to the Inter-Church Mission Education Committee who suggested that I write this book. It is being used as a study document by six denominations: the Anglican Church of Canada, the Christian Church (Disciples of Christ), the Lutheran Church in America – Canada Section, the Presbyterian Church in Canada, the Roman Catholic Church, the United Church of Canada.

Research facilities were generously made available to me by the Parliamentary Librarian, Erik Spicer, and the chief of Parliamentary Research, Philip Laundy. I deeply appreciate their professional courtesies. I am grateful also to Robert Miller, research officer in the Parliamentary Library, who provided background papers on international development.

The Canadian Mission at the United Nations has provided much help to me. I thank Ambassador Saul Rae and the Mission's Minister and Deputy, Permanent Representative, Geoffrey Bruce.

Ruth Fraser, my literary agent, has been a source of continuing guidance.

My secretaries, Pamela Miles and Betty Mitchell, helped in many stages of the manuscript preparation, along with Anne Warren and Edna Clifford.

Ottawa, November 28, 1975